T0161189

PRAISE FOR *INTERRUPTED ENTREPRENEURSHIP*

Raméz A. Baassiri's fine book on Interrupted Entrepreneurship (IE) in family companies is full of EI (emotional intelligence) and wisdom on the management of family firms. Structured around his insightful observations on how to appreciate and address the interruptions in our life paths, Baassiri uses his family's story, and those of many famous families in business, to guide family companies to lasting success.

—Professor John Davis

Chair, Families in Business Program, Harvard Business School

In his book Interrupted Entrepreneurship, *Raméz A. Baassiri manages to weave his own hard-won expertise and knowledge with that of leading scholars and their case studies into a unique, highly accessible, and deeply insightful narrative helping family businesses in all industries and geographies navigate the tumultuous waters of disruptive change.*

—Pascal Finette

Vice President, Startup Solutions, Singularity University

It's been said that corporate responsibility is not how money is spent but how money is made. Raméz A. Baassiri brings to life the reality of keeping the spark of entrepreneurship alive, whilst never forgetting the responsibility expected from those to whom much is given in his book Interrupted Entrepreneurship.

—Dr. Ravi A. Fernando

Executive in Residence, INSEAD Business School, Social Innovation Centre (France), Chairman/CEO-Global Strategic Corporate Sustainability Pvt. Ltd E, Operations Director, Malaysia Blue Ocean Strategy Institute (MBOSI)

The book artfully tackles the thorny issues of navigating family businesses with thoughtful insights on the leadership required for success.

—Niro Sivanathan

Associate professor, London Business School

Raméz's book is a fascinating exploration of the challenges and opportunities that family business such as ours have dealt with over past generations, and presents constructive thoughts on how to approach the future, taking into consideration both advancing technology and the insights of the up-and-coming generation.

—Jason Duff

Vice President, Ohio Ready Mix, Inc. / Duff Quarry

CEO & Founder, Canby Development

Raméz gets to the core of family business as he addresses the rewarding complexities that come with working alongside family, and he highlights that the key to a flourishing family business is the values of the family as much as it is the business itself. He understands the role that family dynamics play in decision-making and the importance of using emotional intelligence to navigate these situations that they forgot to teach us about in business school! If you're a member of a family business, you'll find this book both comforting and educational. You're not alone!

—M. Troy Marcus

General Partner, Mimco, Inc.

I found Interrupted Entrepreneurship *to be a useful roadmap for entrepreneurs as they face struggles in their family businesses. If you have a family business, or are planning to start one, this book provides a helpful and comforting perspective from others who have walked these roads and successfully made it past their own roadblocks.*

—Laura Huang

Assistant professor of management and entrepreneurship at the Wharton School

This book is a tremendous reflection on Ramez's own experiences and observations over continents and generations. It weaves a wonderful fabric of anecdotes and perspectives drawn from other successful businesses around the globe. Writing this book must have been hugely cathartic exercise for him and will serve as a source of inspiration to families who maintain, manage, and mix family with business.

—Jeff Skinner

We acquire considerably more insight when actors from the scene give us their personal perspectives on a topic. Raméz Baassiri does just that for family business scholarships as a family business members in his book Interrupted Entrepreneurship. *The blend of his firsthand experiences weaved in with family business fundamentals are sure to enlighten many readers.*

—Steve Harvey, PhD

Dean, Suliman S. Olayan School of Business, American University of Beirut

INTERRUPTED
ENTREPRENEURSHIP™

INTERRUPTED
ENTREPRENEURSHIP™

EMBRACING CHANGE IN THE
FAMILY BUSINESS

RAMÉZ A. BAASSIRI

ForbesBooks

Published by ForbesBooks, Charleston, South Carolina.
Member of Advantage Media Group.

ForbesBooks is a registered trademark, and the ForbesBooks colophon is a trademark of Forbes Media, LLC.

Printed in the United States of America.

10 9 8 7 6 5 4 3 2

ISBN: 978-1-946633-36-1
LCCN: 2017956179

Cover design by George Stevens.
Layout design by Megan Elger.

This publication is designed to provide accurate and authoritative information in regard to the subject matter covered. It is sold with the understanding that the publisher is not engaged in rendering legal, accounting, or other professional services. If legal advice or other expert assistance is required, the services of a competent professional person should be sought.

 Advantage Media Group is proud to be a part of the Tree Neutral® program. Tree Neutral offsets the number of trees consumed in the production and printing of this book by taking proactive steps such as planting trees in direct proportion to the number of trees used to print books. To learn more about Tree Neutral, please visit **www.treeneutral.com**.

Since 1917, the Forbes mission has remained constant. Global Champions of Entrepreneurial Capitalism. ForbesBooks exists to further that aim by bringing the Stories, Passion, and Knowledge of top thought leaders to the forefront. ForbesBooks brings you The Best in Business. To be considered for publication, please visit **www.forbesbooks.com**.

To Dad, my mentor, whose calm, deep wisdom, tactful planning, and farsighted vision molded my personality.

To Mom, who taught me that I could do anything I put my mind to. She showed me the art of discovery, timing, methodical planning, and the value of principles.

L'ESPRIT D'ENTREPRISE INTERROMPU

broch
nehm
afbrudt

imprenditorialità interrotto

принима

imprenditorialità interrotto

unterbrochen
Unternehmertum

værksa

WHAT IS INTERRUPTED ENTREPRENEURSHIP?

An interruption is anything that causes a break in continuity. It can be a good interruption, such as the birth of a new child, or a bad one, as in the loss of a loved one. The same goes when interruptions occur in business. They can be challenging, such as those interruptions that occur when starting a new business in a foreign land, and they can be beneficial, such as embracing new technology to stay ahead of the competition. In any light, Interrupted Entrepreneurship is just that: moments or actions that cause a change in your business. It's how those IEs are handled that is the key to businesses surviving throughout the generations.

ACKNOWLEDGMENTS

STEVE HARVEY   TRAN TANG PHUONG

NABIL HABAYEB   NIRO SIRVANATHAN   ALEX BRENNAN MARTIN

TEAM MEMBERS   ANA BARATA   NAVIN VALRANI   SANTIAGO SANCHEZ

A. H. BAASSIRI

M. TROY MARCUS

DEMETRI ARGYROPOULO   ADAM WITTY

ZIAD MAKKAWI   LOUAY ABU GHAZALEH

SUZY KANOO

MOHAMMED MOHEBI

SUBRAMANIAN EASSUWAREN

MICHEL FATTAL

PROF. JOHN DAVIS

MY SIBLINGS

YOUNG PRESIDENTS ORGANIZATION & THE MEMBERS OF MY YPO FORUM   MATERNAL GRANDMOTHER   MATERNAL GRANDFATHER

DAD & MOM

FAYE, TALIA & LANA

GUNTER PAULI

JEFF SKINNER

LAURA HUANG

MARTY PARKER   SAAD AND BISTANY FAMILIES   DEVON CAPUR   SINGULARITY UNIVERSITY

MY WIFE

BASEL HAMWI   SAJNA SHAMSUDIN

KC CHAMI   BASSAM SOUEIDAN

CRAIG DUNHAM   AAA/T2T GANG

PASCAL FINETTE

MICHAEL FARR

CRAIG ENENSTEIN

JASON DUFF   PATERNAL GREAT-GRANDMOTHER

MANISH PATEL   CARLITO FUENTE

DR. RAVI A. FERNANDO

TABLE OF CONTENTS

PARDON THE INTERRUPTION

Interruptions within a business are as much a part of life as breathing and blinking—they are viewed by some as hiccups, challenges, or even crises. They are, quite simply, a change in the entrepreneurial experiences of both individuals and within the business itself, and one must be ready to accept and even embrace such changes as they come, to get creative with them, and to use them as a catalyst for improvement. In essence, how we choose to deal with Interrupted Entrepreneurship (or IE) is one of the key qualities that defines our professional, as well as our personal, lives. From dealing with the business cycles of IEs in their many forms, to family transitions, in the end, family businesses ultimately have one question in mind: are we going to engage with these interruptions in entrepreneurship as setbacks or as opportunities?

As a multi-generation family firm that recently experienced the loss of its patriarch and entrepreneurial force, our family felt a major jolt with my father's sudden passing. Along with deep grief, the experience led me to undergo a time of self-reflection and introspection during which I further came to admire my father at every corner, from his leadership, to the farsightedness he had, to envisioning a structure that could survive him. Yet, that seismic change, the interruption that his passing brought about, marked a symbolic fork in the road for our family—one that we strive to handle well as the business he left to us continues to evolve.

Recognizing that what we experienced was just one of many key powerful interruptions that family businesses experience, it led me to question how other enduring family businesses have experienced this and other forms of Interrupted Entrepreneurship and how they have handled it. Did they regroup and defend, rebuild, and expand, or take a whole new road altogether?

On my journey in writing this book, I found that even though there is a full spectrum of business types across every culture and continent in the world, the changes presented through IEs of family business are as tightly interwoven as the threads of a fine silk fabric.

Every family business that has ever existed and, I dare say, will ever exist has dealt and will deal with interruptions, from the expected changes and challenges of growth, to the unexpected interruptions resulting from loss and poor decision-making, and everything in between.

Interrupted Entrepreneurship is not about advice—it's about support. Whether you're a member of a family business, a business owner, a team member, or a family member, I hope that you will find strength in discovering how other family businesses have met—or plan to meet—interruptions in their different forms in business and in life, and how they either overcame or prepared for them.

For me, learning that others have not only dealt with so many changes, some similar to ours, but have also used them to grow has been a source of deep hope and encouragement, and it has given me better insight about the changes our family business may yet still face. That I got a glimpse of how others have walked different roads, weathered the storms, and come out not only intact but stronger shines a new light for me on my own family business's transitions and our agile growth over more than a century by seeking, adapting, and discovering new paths.

So why focus on family business? Today, family businesses are a vital, distinct form of business in the vast majority of countries around the world and make up most of the business types in first world countries and others, with family firms representing 80 percent of all firms in the United States, 85 percent of all firms in the European Union, 90 percent of companies in the Middle East, and 99 percent in Japan, to name a handful.

Despite continental divides and generational differences, I've found that there is a recurring theme of hope in those family businesses that face IE head on. Each chapter of *Interrupted Entrepreneurship* will address several stories of family businesses, providing case studies and lessons learned, and in some instances, a bouquet of paths taken to review and consider.

Of course, this is by no means a one-solution-fits-all book, as we are all unique. Instead, it is intended more as a glimpse into history from which we can derive lessons—and a glimpse into the possibilities from which we can mold our own futures.

Chapters 1–7 of this book take a "zoom-in" approach, looking back at the decisions that have shaped family businesses over the years, while Chapter 8 provides a "zoom-out" perspective, considering the wealth of possibilities that the future holds and how businesses may prosper from acting early on and ahead of the curve.

I hope this book delivers on its core goal and serves as a stepping stone, empowering its readers. I ask anyone who feels they have a story to share that adds to this collective experience to send an e-mail to storIEs@interruptedentrepreneurship.com.

Perhaps this book and future revisions will make more readily available an anecdote or two that will give you the strength and insight you need to face your own family business interruptions and push that success rate of family firms up a few more percentage points—or at a minimum, ease the transition.

L'ESPRIT D'ENTREPRISE INTERROMPU
imprenditorialità interrotta

принима

рерыват

broch
nehm
abrudt

द्या

INTERROM
emprendimiento
interrompida

PRERUSH
HIBRUDI
WERKSATTEN

unterbrochenen
Unternehmertum

værks

राधति उद्यमति

Imprenditorialità interrotto

imprendimiento
interrumpida
werksatten

CHAPTER 1

— • —

Exponential Growth Opportunities in New Horizons

"Small opportunities are often the beginning of great enterprises."
—DEMOSTHENES

In researching this book, it surprised me to learn that even though family firms make up two-thirds[1] of the businesses around the world, they struggle to survive beyond generation one. One can conclude from this that the entrepreneurial spirit is strong, even though the rate of success is diminishing. Studies have shown that only about 30 percent of family firms make this transition successfully, while only 10–15 percent make it to generation three, and only 3–4 percent make it to generation four. What's more, it is estimated that 70 percent of a family's inheritance is lost by the second generation, and 90 percent is gone by the third generation.[2]

---

1   Family Firm Institute Global Data Points, www.ffi.org/page/globaldatapoints

2   Chris Taylor, "70 Percent of Rich Families Lose Their Wealth by the Second Generation," *Reuters*, *Time.com*, June 17, 2015, http://time.com/money/3925308/rich-families-lose-wealth/

That is a statistic that would concern any family business, regardless of what generation you fall in (and as a fourth generation, I should be particularly concerned)! But what I also discovered is that those families that do survive are the ones willing to keep an eye on new horizons. Just because a business model or product has worked in the past doesn't mean it will continue to do so, and while innovative diversification and delving into doing something altogether new could be disruptive, it is also an opportunity to negotiate a new path.

An example of innovation is the German brewery Karlsberg Brauerei,[3] where the company may never have made it into the twenty-first century as a "pure" family-owned business if the owner's son, Christian Weber, hadn't negotiated a new path and pursued the opportunity to stay in the family business—which he almost didn't.

Despite being the great-great-grandson of the brewery's founder, Christian, like many children of family business owners, grew up wanting to get out of his parents' shadow. It wasn't until the company faced an IE—a transition that could strip the company of family ownership—that Christian reached out to his father and proposed a plan in which he succeeded into his father's position. His father ultimately agreed—a transition that I presume took patience, to say the least.

Today, Christian now holds the CEO position at Karlsberg Brauerei. For advice and governance, he turns to his family, including his father, the four family members on his seven-member board, and twenty-five family shareholders, building on their wisdom to help guide the company. Their collective influence at the brewery has resulted in an environment that encourages good ideas above fast decision-making and generates a culture that celebrates innovation.

---

3   *Great Expectations: The Next Generation of Family Business Leaders. PWC report.* April 2016, www.pwc.com/gx/en/family-business-services/publications/assets/next-gen-report.pdf

Karlsberg Brauerei is now one of the largest breweries in Germany.[4] In this case, Christian stuck it out, negotiated a new path that was inclusive of the old guard—his father and family members—and has driven company growth while staying true to the core business.

For instance,[5] by collaborating with international breweries and expanding on their artisan and craft beers, offering limited-edition and special craft brews both through distributors and online, Karlsberg celebrated a notably successful 2016. In fact, while Weber is excited about the potential for more new products in coming years, he also faces the problem of limited capacity at the current plant. It's a good interruption to have, but one that he and the family will need to confront soon in order to move forward.

When you look at the threads of family business from the perspective of decades, or even centuries—akin to marveling at a vast tapestry of design, characters, and influences—you see how the threads weave together to form that most fundamental layer of beauty: a pattern.

For multigenerational family businesses, the most basic and inherently enduring pattern is *survival.*

In this chapter, we will explore what survival means in family businesses. For some generations, survival means migration; for others, growth, innovation, reinvention, and even disruption. Here, we'll look at four multigenerational families—the Piedimonte family, the Kalmoni family, the Brooke family, as well as our own family—who survived to generation three, four, and beyond.

---

4   https://en.wikipedia.org/wiki/Karlsberg_(brewery)

5   Joachim Wollschlager, "Brauerei Karlsberg geht mit der Brau-Mode," *sol.de,* Nov. 12, 2016. www.sol.de/neo/nachrichten/saarbruecken/Brauerei-Karlsberg-geht-mit-der-Brau-Mode;art34275,4811468

Opportunity on the Horizon

For my family, our path to growth began with migration when my ancestors moved outwards from Lebanon to what must have seemed like the end of the world.

Fortunately, they weren't alone. Citizens of the Levant area had been emigrating in a steady stream for quite some time, with a boost occurring in 1860 following a sudden collapse in the silk trade.

But as the saying goes, one man's loss is another man's gain. My great-grandfather, A. H. Baassiri, along with other family members and compatriots saw the opportunities South America, Africa, etc. were presenting to hundreds of thousands of Lebanese and decided to make the journey in the hopes of building a new and better life for his young family. It helped, too, that he was undertaking this journey during the height of the Industrial Revolution. Travel by all means of transportation, from boat, to train, to the newly invented airplane and automobile, was making travel faster and cheaper—a benefit not only to those wishing to see the world but to build new business based on these increasingly productive and soon-to-be-cost-efficient factors.

That decision was the beginning of our family branch's evolution as "global citizens." As the world opened up through transportation and technology, we grew with it, flowing outward and adapting our business cycles. And as the Industrial Revolution progressed, we continued to grow with it, modeling new ventures around these waves of innovation, from the early stages of mechanization to mass production, computers and automation, and today seeking to keep up with the latest in cyber-physical systems (for more on forward thinking, see Chapter 8).

Under A. H. Baassiri's leadership and the leadership of other family members—including my late father, former chairman Abdul

Hamid Baassiri, as well as other members of our generation and hopefully generations that may follow—our family business was able to put down roots across multiple continents and multiple generations.

Migration and the Launch of the Family Business

A small but strong Lebanese community seemed to form across these newly migrated-to cities in the early 1900s when some of my ancestors and other families arrived, which was likely a strong reason they chose to move there at the time. Having at least some small connection to home made it easier to adjust and grow in a foreign land. In later years, through the spectacles of exploration that were placed on us by my mother, we saw diversity in the new and unknown, which made it easier to navigate and in turn gave us the true foundation needed to become global citizens.

In fact, this pattern of migration—where a small number of immigrants find successful work in a new land and eventually send for their families, drawing relations and friends to the same area to build businesses and a community—is so prevalent that it is known as "chain migration," [6] and it is a pattern that many others have followed when confronted with hardships in their home country or when seeking better opportunities somewhere else.

Some say timing is everything, but it's not. Whether it's being in the right place at the right time or coming across just the right product for that exact moment in history, timing is only part of it. Our family may have been in the right place at the right time for becoming involved in the trade industry, just as the Industrial Revolution was spurring on the building of new roads and railroads, but

---

6   Laura Hougaz, *Entrepreneurs in Family Business Dynasties: Stories of Italian-Australian Family Businesses over 100 Years* (New York: Springer International Publishing, 2015).

they were also keen to get on board with new technology at the head of the curve. It's not just about timing but about keeping an eye out for those new paths and innovations that could send you hurtling into the future (for more on forward thinking in the modern era, see Chapter 8).

The Opportunity for Migration during Colonial Expansion

Between the late nineteenth century and early twentieth century, as world powers such as Great Britain, Japan, the Ottoman Empire, and the Soviet Union fought to expand their reach and acquire new territories during the era of New Imperialism,[7, 8] the rate of migration exploded. With new roads and railroads being built, and the improvement of ocean travel as well as the rapid population growth in Europe, migration reached some of it's highest levels in history.

We have all heard the saying, "It was tougher in the olden days." Wars, famine, and disputes were exponentially worse back then than they are today. According to a 2013 report by the Human Security Report Project, "In the 1950s, there were almost 250 deaths caused by war per million people. Now there are less than 10 per million."[9] The report goes on to state, "It's easy to forget how dangerous life used to be, how deeply brutality was once woven into the fabric of daily existence."

In Italy, many of the country's citizens had become tired of the feudal *mezzadria* agricultural system (where peasants cultivated the land of the landlord in exchange for a percentage of the produce grown) and sought new opportunities in other lands. Between 1861 and the 1970s,

---

7   https://en.wikipedia.org/wiki/New_Imperialism#Motivation

8   http://www2.sunysuffolk.edu/westn/imperialism.html

9   http://www.hsrgroup.org/docs/Publications/HSR2013/HSRP_Report_2013_
        140226_Web.pdf

almost 30 million Italians left their homeland for other countries, with a small but significant number finding their way to Australia.

Figures for the Human Security Report 2013

Figure 5.2 Global Trends in Battle Deaths from State-Based Conflicts, 1946–2008

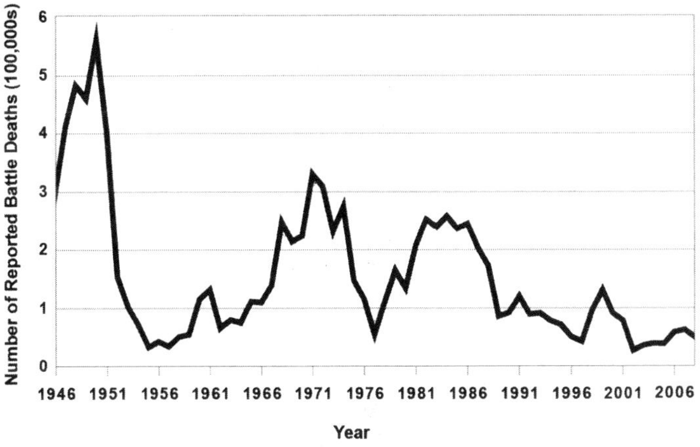

Battle deaths peaked in 1950 due to the Korean War, in the 1970s due to the Vietnam War, and in the 1980s due to the Iran-Iraq and Afghanistan wars. Despite these deadly wars, battle deaths have declined since 1946.

Data Source: PRIO.

One of these was the Piedimonte family, led by Giuseppe Piedimonte, who emigrated from Italy to Australia in 1950.[10] Sponsored by an uncle already living in Melbourne, Giuseppe followed the familiar pattern of chain migration and moved to the country ahead of his family, working in a wool mill warehouse for years, until he saved up enough to sponsor his wife and two sons to come to the country. In 1958, the Piedimonte family opened their own business, an Italian delicatessen called Piedimonte & Sons.

After so many years of working for others, this business was their opportunity to build something for themselves. And even though

10   Hougaz, *Entrepreneurs.*

each of them had to deal with the IE of working full-time jobs outside of running the family store for more than a year, that sacrifice proved to benefit the family many times over—one such benefit being the knowledge gained while working outside of the business.

When the family business moved into generation two, they had saved enough to purchase the tailor shop next door and expanded their offerings to include imported Italian products, including oils, pastas, and cheeses. By the 2010s, after their third expansion, the company has two locations and trades under the IGA (Independent Grocers of Australia) banner, with the third generation of Piedimontes serving in key management roles.

It took traveling to a new land and years of dedication and hardships, but the Piedimontes were able to overcome significant interruptions and stay true to their goal of one day running a successful business that would survive for generations to come.

It was this same mentality that A. H. Baassiri embraced as he faced the interruption of starting another family business in a foreign land. Fortunately, he saw opportunity in how trade and transportation was not only encouraging growth within the region but also across continents, as overseas transportation, too, was becoming quicker and more efficient. With that in mind, he now turned his focus toward the potentials of trade and growth within the new burgeoning economy of Africa.

Opportunity in Africa

It was still early in the twentieth century, during the era known as "the Scramble for Africa,"[11] when A. H. Baassiri decided to seek better opportunities in the rapidly industrializing African continent.

---

11   http://www.joh.cam.ac.uk/library/library_exhibitions/schoolresources/exploration/
    scramble_for_africa/

At the time, several European countries as well as the United States were grabbing up African territories as fast as they could in the hopes of benefitting from the country's vast quantities of raw materials. It was a time of violent conflict, but also of growth, as Europeans saw the country as another opportunity for growth and migrated to Africa by the thousands.

A. H. once again set his sights on foreign lands, this time looking toward Africa, which had also seen a large influx of Lebanese over the past several decades.

The possibilities for growth in Africa in the early 1900s were just as strong, if not stronger, in the French-controlled Ivory Coast and Senegal, as well as British-controlled Ghana. Immigration to these areas was encouraged, but it was also a forced arrival for many, as steam-powered ships on their way across the Atlantic would either dock in Senegal or be blown off course and be forced to land in Senegal or the Ivory (then "Gold") Coast. According to second-generation Lebanese businessman Nouhad Kalmoni,[12] "My grandfather's brother was originally going to America. They got on the ship and were dropped off at the Gold Coast. People here said to them, 'Welcome to America!'"

Kalmoni's family migration to Africa, like many other family businesses at the time, followed a similar pattern to my great-grandfather's. Both of our families arrived on the continent around the same time, although Kalmoni landed in Tripoli, while we found opportunity starting on the west coast of Africa, where both families eventually became involved in the transportation business. Though it probably didn't strike them as humorous at the time, I smile a little at the irony of how some families back then almost became lost at

---

12   http://www.aljazeera.com/programmes/aljazeeraworld/2015/10/lebanon-
      africa-151027114653139.html

sea and were driven to live in an unexpected land (a pretty significant IE!), only later to become involved in the business of navigation and transportation as they guided others and products to their final destination.

Today, the Kalmoni family, now in its third generation, is heavily involved in several industries in Ghana, including real estate and the automotive sector, with their Silver Star Auto LTD company considered the largest dealer in Mercedes-Benz in Ghana.[13]

As for the Baassiri family, for some time we became involved in a variety of activities including trade and transportation, bringing new innovations and new industries under our family business umbrella.

But all the while, we kept a base of sorts in the home country, in part because A. H. wanted to keep ties with the land he loved, exporting goods and ideas back, and keeping the wheel of trade turning.

Then, just as the wave of emigration from Lebanon took our family across oceans and continents in the early 1900s, it brought us back to the Levant in the 1930s/40s. It was here that we rerouted our business interests yet again and acquired land in the Levant area and began trading.

Fortunately, my great-grandfather's experience in the numerous industries across continents provided him with the knowledge of how to successfully transport and export a variety of commodities, to the point where he then focused on using Mann Trucks exclusively within his logistics operation. Mann afforded him the ability to transport goods without paying a middleman and also provided another income source through the commercial trading of Mann trucks, all the way up to his passing in the mid-1950s.

---

13   http://ghanavibes.com/photo-12-filthy-richest-people-ghana-2/4/

Between international trading and running a logistics set up—along with several other enterprises, including Michelin Tires—A. H. also had another standalone business that was particularly close to his heart: cinema houses.

THE WORLD THROUGH DIFFERENT SPECTACLES

For as long as I'd known him, my father had a remarkably strong focus on the future. Rarely did he speak about the past unless it was to share a lesson or to strengthen ties (this book is based on this idea). Life was not meant to be lived in the past but to be lived with hope and joy and great expectations for the future.

One day, however, he told me a sweet, short little story about how, as a boy, he loved to go to the cinema. Since his family operated two cinema houses in town, he had his own special seat and as a teen would go as often as he could.

Of course, this was the 1950s, when the Silver Screen was arguably at its finest, and going to the movies was an event in itself. The Golden Age, he said, is an example that not all was terrible in the olden days. But his story held a whole other meaning to me, to learn that in his youth he had such passion for the movies and the big screen. *The apple doesn't fall far from the tree*, I said to myself.

It was a connection that I never realized I had with him. I love going to the movies, as well, but I didn't think he would relate to me. I didn't want to be judged for spending time at the movies when I could be conducting business or spending more time with my family. To hear him say it, however, spoke to me—it suddenly explained a part of me and connected me not only to my father but to my great-grandfather, who created the cinemas as a business to start with. It was a passion and love that I'd inherited without knowing it until now. How important to share sometimes the smallest of things … it is those things that carry the most weight for decades, if not for a lifetime.

It is amazing how a few words can share a lifetime of experiences. This is one reason why I recommend that each of us be open and share with our team members and loved ones. There has to be a balance between what is said and unsaid, but some things are best said, such as the time shortly before my dad's passing when he said to me, "I love you, but I can't find the words to express how much I respect you … ." I'll carry these words with me always, knowing I am one of the lucky ones who got to appreciate my relationship not only with my boss but also with my father. In fact, a dear friend of mine, Navin Valrani, had these words engraved on a plaque, which I keep in a place of honor in my home.

The cinema is about the beauty of imagination and creation. It is about stepping outside of your world, thinking outside of your box—I would even go so far as to say coming outside of your mental prison—and realizing that there is a horizon beyond your own horizon. It changes your mood and invigorates you in a way that only the possibility of limitless possibilities can.

It wasn't so much the fact that my father, grandfather, great-grandfather, and even my maternal grandfather loved the movies—it was that we shared this interest in the ability to see the world through different spectacles and found success in doing what they loved, and loving what they did.

When my great-grandfather passed away, the cinemas died with him, as did many of the industries he became involved in, as the entrepreneurial spirit struggled to survive in the next generation, though the processes and opportunities they all afforded carried on. Fortunately, the real estate investments he'd made served as a life raft for our family as we survived the political growth interruption of the entire region and generation.

Engineering Change

"Live what you love and love what you do. Hone your skills toward what you love to excel in."
—MY FATHER, ABDUL HAMID BAASSIRI

There are no limits for reinventing yourself. This philosophy has been expressed in one form or another from Sartre's assertion, "If man … is indefinable, it is because at first he is nothing. Only afterward will he be something, and he himself will have made what he will be," to Heraclitus's statement, "The only thing that is constant is change." No matter what, we all must be prepared to deal with change by being ready to embrace the future and grow with it instead of refusing to acknowledge the inevitable: that change will come, whether or not we're ready for it. This is a philosophy I share with and explore in many a conversation with my dear friends, Michel Fattal and Manish Patel.[14]

With that in mind, my father's words ring as true to me today as they ever did, and I believe that philosophy played a big role in the change of the nature of our business as my father turned his business focus toward a personal passion that, at the time, was also very forward thinking: engineering.

---

14   Michel Fattal, Manish Patel, and other forum member peers have served me well over the years, providing me with insight and the ability to engage with very diverse points of view and experiences.

That philosophy also extended to his siblings, who chose to pursue higher studies in their respective passions in medical and educational fields. My patriarch's path led him to seek knowledge of enterprise and world business by working outside for a longer time than anticipated, working for a multinational company and gaining that mind-set and structure. In his case, it helped him to evolve an agile mind and allow for more fluid structure.

A lot of family business leaders will tell you that their company survived on traits such as ingenuity, frugality, and the strength of the family bond, but they'll also tell you that luck played a pretty big part, as well. For my father, it was a combination of some of these factors that came into play when the opportunity to get involved in a number of new areas of business presented themselves.

The family, along with a number of partners along the way, got into numerous other businesses over time. We diversified, evolving our business model to reflect exponential, rather than linear thinking, investing, and spinning one business into the next, always seeking growth in some form or fashion, carrying the expertise we'd gained from one and expanding into another. In each enterprise, each a standalone entity, we learned something new and then built on that, refining the knowledge over years and decades, working that DNA into our company systems.

Growth through Passion

Like his grandfather before him, Abdul Hamid didn't just diversify in the Gulf Cooperation Council states, [15] either. He expanded with investments across neighboring continents, and reinvigorated investment connections that grew businesses in Africa and Asia, expanding

---

15   As of 2017, the GCC consisted of member states: Bahrain, Kuwait, Oman, Qatar, Saudi Arabia, and the United Arab Emirates (UAE).

the company's geographic footprint exponentially. He became involved in manufacturing, trading, services, and real estate, capitalizing not just on entrepreneurial opportunity but also on the fact that the United Arab Emirates (UAE) was quickly becoming an international hub, geared toward cultivating the entrepreneurial spirit by exemplary leadership.

Change in the demand for products or services is an interruption that every family business—and every business—will face. Some businesses have come and gone, of course, and those experiences have helped us to evolve while at the same time helping the present businesses grow strong. Our family embraced change (a core value that we held close to our hearts before and after my father passed away) by investing in and developing businesses, both internal and external, that built on the same common core values, such as loyalty and trust and transparency, and the methodical processes he created, while still allowing those businesses to be independent parts in a greater concentric circle of growth. The concept of values cannot be stressed enough. I try every day to live the values that my parents taught me, and I do my best to pass those on to the next generation—my three daughters.

For our generation, as it is for others, that change may come in an entirely new form of industry, such as the change that the Brooke family business underwent in the late 1980s.

"Each generation should be encouraged to develop the business consistent with his own skills and interests," said Mark Brooke, company chairman of John Brooke & Sons Holdings LTD during an interview.[16]

Founded in 1541, Brooke & Sons has been recognized as the United Kingdom's oldest existing family business. For more than

---

16   William T. O'Hara, *Centuries of Success: Lessons from the World's Most Enduring Family Businesses* (New York: Adams Media Corporation, 2004), 70.

four hundred years and over the course of fifteen generations, the company was a renowned provider of quality woolen textiles. Following World War II and the emergence of cotton and synthetic fabrics, however, the woolen textiles industry took a downturn from which it never recovered.

Faced with the IE of the long, slow death of an industry, the family business survived due to a stroke of innovation by its present-day chairman, Mark Brooke, who chose not to look at what the family business did but also at the elements it had available.

While his father, Edward Brooke, had difficulty letting go of the family's past in woolen textiles, Mark saw their company's physical space—a 200,000-square-foot industrial mill complex—as an opportunity. In the late 1990s, several years after the last mill under the family's name had closed shop, Mark reopened the mill as the Yorkshire Technology and Office Park, a renovated complex featuring sections of the mill completely transformed into bright office spaces for small companies involved in everything from software to health care to financial services.

The complex has been so successful that Mark is now looking to other mills that could be converted to small business use, though Mark has stressed that any renovation his company takes on will follow the Brooke's way. That is, they will only be top-end, high-quality conversions that will rank them far and above any competitors.

In his interview with O'Hara, Mark pointed out, "This [the Brooke's former mill] isn't a museum, but a living, working space with the capacity to play a new role as a reinvented family business in the twenty-first century."

It is this "first principle" approach of looking at the foundational elements of a business and seeing a new direction based on what's available that propels family businesses into the future, supporting them during lulls in business cycles and the uncertainty of growth and change, and launching them in the direction of forward, future success.

Brooke & Sons is just one example of how one is always faced with change, especially when the question of a business's viability is at stake. In thinking disruptively—that is, by challenging the status quo and making bold moves, not bound by what just others may think— you not only open up the opportunity to reinvent your business but also your own way of thinking.

For us, looking at a cross-section of the past century of entrepreneurship and innovation, we moved from land cultivation to engineering over multiple generations. It was the interruptions that allowed for a revamping of the nature of our business for the better. As the Brooke family did, we reached a full cycle and began again, building on the core values of the past.

Build on Your Core

From experience, I suggest that you don't have to know everything there is to know about a particular business or industry to invest in it. If someone came to me and said, "Invest in chocolates," the first thing that would come to mind is that I don't know anything about chocolates (although ironically, the first business I ever took on as a personal venture was a chocolate business with a Belgian entrepreneur).

But that wouldn't stop me if I thought there was potential in the idea. There are key core elements one ought to know, such as how to evaluate a business balance sheet, how to review a marketing plan, how to do an advertising process, etc. And understanding that human resources (some might add A. I., which I discuss in Chapter

8) are key, and managing them well is vital in any business. You need to have that core knowledge that can be carried from one business or industry to another. Constantly educating and reeducating yourself is an invaluable quality when it comes to growing business—a topic I speak more on in the chapter on education (Chapter 6).

In understanding that we have this core knowledge in how to run businesses and invest in businesses that feed into each other and support each other, my father created a corporate structure that could survive him, that wouldn't bottleneck at one person but would instead allow us to build on our passions and core knowledge while still growing the family business. It also further ensured that the next generations would learn to engage as members of a larger group while still exercising their independence. As part of that structure, my parents created the Baassiri Investment Fund so that members of our family would collectively be able to engage in new business ventures of their own interest, allowing for creativity without affecting the core business, and so that they would have something to support them should they fall on hard times. The fund is insulated from the fortunes of the main business, a strategy similar to how Steve Jobs isolated his Macintosh team early on, separating them from Apple so that their concept for Mac would be entirely unique and successful in its own right. (For more about fund creation, see Chapter 4.)

In an interview by family business researcher Loura Hougaz,[17] Joseph Piedimonte, third generation of the successful family-owned grocery business in Australia, spoke to building his family business while staying true to its core.

"The [Italian] customer base that we had has largely moved out of the area, and there's a different customer base now. So, that gave us

---

17   Hougaz, *Entrepreneurs*, 237.

the opportunity to sell new products to this new customer base that was willing to try new and different products."

They stuck with their core strengths, but by growing outward into new markets, they were able to grow their business significantly.

With the Brooke family, too, by following their family's original strengths as traders rather than what they eventually wound up doing—manufacturing—the present generation has been able to successfully seek its own path while still relying on the family business's core strengths.

Family Growth: Cultivating Entrepreneurs

Another inevitable IE of growth is that of the family. You can't have a family business without family members (even if a family business is a corporation or is publicly traded)! Where the challenge lies is in managing these multiple numbers of generational demands and making sure everyone is heard and represented.

We are fortunate to have a comparatively small family nucleus at generation four that revolves around a well-structured and organized system of governance. When it came to growth and expansion of interests in our family, we made sure there was parallel growth of the size and interests of our business alongside it.

Since my father chose to follow a different path than his family business at the time, taking up engineering while still making his interests work to the benefit of the family business, he wanted to make sure other family members had the same opportunity. "Do something else," he said to me. "Follow your heart. You don't have to go into engineering because I did."

This was the beginning of the Baassiri Investment Fund, which allows us to find our own paths toward creating a successful company while potentially shifting the core of the family business. It is a construct of family business that has worked well for many others, including the family-owned Hero Group in India.

Founded as a bicycle manufacturer in the 1950s,[18] the Hero Group grew to become a major manufacturer of bikes by the 1980s— big enough to grab the attention of Honda, who chose the Hero Group over several other competitors to manufacture its motorbikes. Today, the Hero Group makes close to seven million motorcycles a year and is still a solid family business, with five representatives of the current generation working under the Hero umbrella.

These five family members, however, aren't exactly in motorcycle manufacturing. They were each given the same opportunity—to come up with a business idea that appealed to their own interests. As long as they met certain criteria, they were given the freedom and faith to grow their business and, thus, grow the Hero Group.

For third generation Abhimanyu Munjal, that business idea didn't come easily. Upon graduating from university, he worked for two international banks before returning to the family business with the idea of starting an insurance business. Unfortunately, the concept never panned out. Then, after working for some time in the company's auto components division, he found his passion in a "next-generation" approach to financial services. Four years later, Abhimanyu's start-up, Hero Fincorp, has proven to be very successful.

Sometimes, however, the option of starting a smaller business under the family umbrella isn't an option. Sometimes the creativity and innovation of the newest generation is all that stands between success and failure.

With Brooke & Sons, chairman Mark Brooke observed, "You need to understand your own talents" when it comes to family

---

18   *Great Expectations.*

business.[19] For the Brooke family's textile industry, that creative direction was in pursuing a reinvention of the family business that played to Mark's innovative, idea-driven talents while also allowing the family business to thrive. Today, the Brooke name still stands for quality, but that quality has moved from top-tier woolen textiles to superior renovations of architecture to fit today's quality small business needs.

No matter what the course or who is embarking on it—whether it is a company CEO driving in a single, new, and cutting-edge direction, or a family member taking a chance on a new division of business—it is vital that he or she has the capability and know-how to make it work. Education, no matter if it's through experience, higher learning, or a combination thereof, is immeasurably important and is the best way to cultivate positive and beneficial growth. (Read more about education in Chapter 6.)

Values: Cultivating the Land You're Given

A thought that has occurred to every person who has ever taken up the reins of a family business, whether it's the second generation or the forty-fifth, is not just, "Am I going to be successful at this?" but, "Will I be able to maintain this business well enough just to say I didn't screw it up?" Or even dare to ask, "What incredible innovation can I bring to my business?"

And do you ever really know? It is an intangible question. Even when you pass the reins on to the next generation, you still look at it and say, "Did it really succeed as much as it could? Would the generation before me or after me have done better?"

---

19   O'Hara, *Centuries of Success*, 70.

No family business leader is unique in asking this, nor are family businesses as a whole unique in asking this. We all ask this question at some point in our lives. Did we do our best? Did we do as well as earlier generations would have done?

Take the Hoshi Ryokan, a traditional Japanese inn that is considered to be one of the oldest businesses in the world and is now in its forty-sixth generation of family ownership. Founded in 718, the traditional Japanese family business has traditionally followed the rule that only the eldest son can assume ownership.

"Ever since I was born and first cried, everyone told me I will take over Hoshi Ryokan," said Zengoro Houshi, forty-sixth-generation owner of the inn and the forty-sixth "Zengoro Houshi" in his family's history.

"Hoshi Ryokan has been operating for 1,300 years," said Zengoro Houshi in a short documentary by *The Atlantic*.[20] "To keep this ryokan in this ever-changing world, that's our priority."

The tradition of male ownership of the inn faced an IE in 2013 when Zengoro Hoshi's son passed away. Afterward, his single daughter, Hisae, was reluctant to marry someone just because the family deemed him qualified to be adopted and inherit the Zengoro Houshi name and ownership. Instead, she began taking on responsibilities and, despite tradition and her hesitation at filling her father's shoes, her father believed she was the right person to keep the business running and has since turned the ownership of the hotel over to her.[21]

"I now have many unimaginable responsibilities," said Hisae. "It's a heavy burden on my mind." (For more on Gender Empowerment, see Chapter 7.)

---

20   www.theatlantic.com/video/index/387649/this-japanese-inn-has-been-open-for-1300-years/ "This Japanese Inn has been open for 1,300 years."

21   Joanna Prisco, "Japanese Inn Has Been Passed Down 46 Generations," *ABC News*, March 20, 2015, http://abcnews.go.com/Travel/japanese-inn-passed-46-generations/story?id=29782733

In the end, all we can know is this: You can't live trying to fill the footsteps of those who went before you. I only learned this after my dad passed away. He was a larger-than-life person, whose shade encompassed many, and I was one of those who took comfort in that shade. All I can do is live the values that my parents taught me and teach those values to my children, and continue them in our business while seeking to move ahead.

Will I be able to leave my children with more financial security than my father left me when he passed away? Will they live the kind of life I lived? I wish for them the best I ever got and more, if that is possible.

But again, these are intangible questions that can only be answered by how well you live your values. Values are reflected in everything: from your principles, to how you maintain your customer relationships, to how you care for one another, to how you run your business overall.

For the Piedimonte family in Australia who overcame the IE of homeland hardships and migration to create a successful family business, the value of trust is sacred. According to Joseph Piedimonte, "Trust, as you know, is extremely important. You need the help of others, and you need to trust them, as well. This is the soul of family business."[22]

The above statement rang true when my father passed away. As a family, we sought and depended on one another. When you have good values, solid values, people recognize that. It's often what differentiates a family business from a non-family one. That trust not only creates a sense of unity and greater bond between team members, but it also serves as the rich soil in which loyalty, mutual respect, honesty, and a sense of responsibility can grow.

---

22   Hougaz, *Entrepreneurs*, 219–220.

When a family business grows, it is because the family members aren't looking at it as a cow to milk but as a whole farm that they can work together—a farm that can be cultivated, cared for, and grown to the next level.

I subscribe to trust as a fertile soil and hope our team feels the same way.

CHAPTER 2

Celebrating Your Assets

"Money comes and goes. It's what's inside of you that's important—what you have invested in yourself, in your soul, that gets you to the next phase of life."
—ABDUL HAMID BAASSIRI

Our family business weathered rapid changes in the late 1950s due to the nationalizing of properties in the region generally, and in the Levant area specifically, including our own.

The ever-changing geographical landscape over the past few centuries has played an interesting role in our family's history; and history, as we all know, has a way of repeating itself. This is just one of the reasons why it is so important to find a way in your own time to share the stories of your past, personal and professional, with other family members, so that they can learn from your trials, tribulations, and persistence. Even as I write this, I realize that this is yet another thread that ties me to my predecessors in a pattern woven across our individual lives. There is something about knowing the journey of your ancestors when you're traveling a new path: It feels like it is a familiar place, even though it's a place where you personally have never been.

Fortunately, the physical real estate assets that were not nationalized in the 1950s—a governmental act that had a detrimental impact on land accessibility—provided a sustainable base for our family for years to come. My father, Abdul, used his business acumen to focus on a whole new rising phoenix at the time—the Gulf area—by seeking a new path of innovative reengineering from the past family business activities.

Acting on Innovation (Creativity Is a Valuable Asset)

There is a difference between being a dreamer and being an entrepreneur. Many have brilliant ideas; the key is how you overcome that IE by taking your idea and acting on it, nurturing it, toiling over it, and growing it into a reality and, thus, a viable business. What is important is finding a way to make the theory into a reality.

The Jacuzzi family, for instance, emigrated from Italy to Berkeley, California, in the early 1900s, eventually saving enough money from their hard labor as fruit pickers to open a small machine shop further north, in the San Francisco Bay Area.[23] They began by manufacturing various items, including airplane propellers, and even designed the first enclosed cabin plane.

But aeronautics wasn't where the Jacuzzis finally found their foothold. Tireless inventors, the Jacuzzi brothers also created a new kind of water pump that quickly lifted large quantities of water. The pumps sold so well that the brothers focused solely on pump manufacturing until 1956, when the Jacuzzis developed a home-use

---

23   www.jacuzzi.co.uk/jacuzzi-world/history

hydrotherapy pump to treat young Ken Jacuzzi's debilitating juvenile rheumatoid arthritis.

The small SCUBA tank-sized pump was originally built as a side project to help the little boy, but Ken's doctor was so impressed by how well it worked that he recommended that the Jacuzzis manufacture it and sell it to anyone in need of in-home hydrotherapy.

That idea launched the brand, and Jacuzzi pump sales took off, selling incredibly well until the 1960s, when Roy Jacuzzi saw even more potential in their family's asset. Instead of selling separate tanks, he developed a way to build jets into the walls of a tub, and with that, the Jacuzzis transcended innovation and practically launched an industry and are now a common household name.

The Jacuzzi's story represents well the two main forms of assets: tangible and intangible. The creativity of the Jacuzzi family is a valuable intangible asset, and the tangible assets that resulted from it—utility patents and design patents involving the Jacuzzi pump—became foundations on which the Jacuzzi family built its long-term business. Patents, in and of themselves, are an important part of a family business's intellectual property assets and can be a significant part of supporting the long-term survival and growth of family business.

According to Mr. Luay Abu Ghazaleh, the CEO-managing partner of Abu-Ghazaleh Intellectual Property and vice president of Talal Abu-Ghazaleh Organization, intangible assets can be of greater long-term value than tangible assets because intangible assets last for longer periods of time. For example, a patent for a new technology could continue to generate revenues for decades, while the products associated with that patent might have value in inventory for a much shorter amount of time.

"Consider the patent portfolio for IBM," said Ghazaleh. "For twenty-four years in a row, IBM led the US market in the number of patents obtained. It is the first company to break the 8,000 mark in one year with 8,088 patents earned in 2016, and accumulated 97,040 total patents between 1993 and 2017. The net carrying amount of IBM's patents and trademarks was $335 million in 2012, and it has doubled in only one year to become $730 million in 2016.[24]

"Indeed, a company with a well-managed intellectual property portfolio can increase its value, and capturing possible intellectual property assets at the right time and in the right manner can turn a business into an empire worth billions of dollars."

Roy Jacuzzi saw this potential in his family's intellectual property, choosing to see these valuable assets not as something to simply live off of but as resources that could be developed into something greater.

Assets in business come in varying forms as we will describe in this chapter; they are not cows to be milked dry, as stated earlier, but rather are *gardens* that need to be carefully tended, nurtured, and planted with the prospect of years, decades, even centuries of growth in mind—a philosophy that my sister Rim subscribes to strongly.

We often think of assets as tangible goods, like buildings, products, and services, and even the aforementioned cow. But would you consider *entrepreneurial spirit* an asset to your family business?

Perhaps even more important than tangible assets are those that are *in*tangible, such as intellect, business acumen, the ability to communicate well, and the solid set of values that you run your business by.

In today's evolving technology, as well, innovations across the board follow the same rule, falling across the broad range of tangible and intangible. While this chapter addresses a number of examples

---

24   2016 IBM Annual Report, https://www.ibm.com/annualreport/2016/images/downloads/IBM-Annual-Report-2016.pdf

of both tangible and intangible assets that can benefit your family business, we'll talk more about the growth of technology in Chapter 8.

Consider your assets, both tangible and intangible, as the abounding flora you choose to plant in the garden of your life. What you wish to harvest from it determines what you need to plant. You plant different seeds to reach different goals, and each type of plant needs different kinds of nurturing and comes to fruition at different times. When allowed to wither and die, untended assets can end a multigenerational family business. But when nurtured, they can be the very reason for a generation's survival into the next cycle of family business.

Tangible Assets

Real Estate: Land ownership is a leading asset

When I look back on my family's experiences in building our business from Generation One to today, I realize that our progress through interrupted entrepreneurship, with all of its hills and valleys, is not unique.

For the past one hundred years, one of our most powerful assets has been real estate. It was our savior when our business cycles were affected by transitions ranging from political to economical, where at that time so many of what I understand to be our revenue streams were put on hold. The previous generation counted on its land and our properties, and from this source we were able to generate alternative income.

Land ownership is a leading asset for many family businesses, from second-generation business owner Ted Turner's two-million-plus acres in New Mexico[25] to James, Arthur, and John Irving, heirs

---

25   Thornton McEnery, "The World's 15 Biggest Landowners" *Business Insider*, March 18, 2011, www.businessinsider.com/worlds-biggest-landowners-2011-3?op=1

of the J. D. Irving, LTD empire, who own close to four million acres of land between Canada's New Brunswick and Nova Scotia and the state of Maine.[26] It is a tangible asset that should be built into any business model, not only because of the land's inherent value but also because of its stability and versatility. However, it is important not to underplay that it is also a finite asset. Simply, when you have land, you can create a revenue stream from it, whether you sell, lease it, use it as collateral, or build on it.

Take London's Grosvenor family, which acquired five hundred acres "of swamp, pasture, and orchards" just west of London in 1677 as a result of the marriage of Mary Davies and Sir Thomas Grosvenor.[27] Some 350 years later, the Grosvenors still own three hundred of those acres, now located in well-known subdivisions of London, including Belgravia and Mayfair—home to Grosvenor Square.

Applying centuries of knowledge of real estate holdings and development, the Grosvenor family expanded outside of the United Kingdom in the mid-twentieth century, undertaking development projects in Australia, the Americas, and Continental Europe. Today, the family is involved in real estate in sixty cities around the world and continues to grow, while remaining a family-owned, privately held entity.

Property Ownership: One of the oldest symbols of wealth

Property ownership is one of the world's oldest symbols of wealth, and as a tangible asset, if it is clean and clear of liabilities, it can become a real nest egg. Initially, some acquired it and protected it, as the Grosvenor family did, and if they had enough to allow others to live on it, that land became an asset, generating income and con-

---

26   www.therichest.com/rich-list/the-biggest/12-of-the-biggest-land-owners-on-earth/

27   www.grosvenor.com/about-grosvenor/

sequently boosting them to a leadership position in the community. Those looking to move up in the world also found ways to claim their own land for the same reasons. Landowners not only gained wealth through tenancy and taxation but also through the inherent power of their position.

The Van der Merwe family of South Africa is an excellent example of land ownership facilitating the survival of the family business for centuries.[28]

Willem Van der Merwe was the first of his family to arrive in South Africa in 1660, working as a guard for the Dutch East India Company in the Cape of Good Hope. It wasn't until 1743, however, that his family became involved in agriculture when Willem's grandson, Izaak, leased a land area he called Modder Valley from the Dutch East India Company. It was another seventy years before the family gained complete ownership of the land, but once in their hands, the family was able to live off of it for generations and continues to do so today.

Even though portions of the land have been subdivided over the years, the family still commands more than two thousand acres, focusing on an intense cultivation of apples and pears. The main farmland is known as Boplaas, or "high farm," and their more recent acquisition is called Wadrif, or "wagon crossing."

Through changes in government (such as in our family's case, as well), the impacts of apartheid, and the wild unpredictability of nature, the Van der Merwes have an undying faith not only in the strength of their farm but also in the strength of their family. Trust, as I have mentioned before, is sacred, and an invaluable asset in any form of relationship—be it God, nature, business, or family.

---

28   O'Hara, *Centuries of Success.*

I can certainly appreciate the role that cultivating land can play in one's life.

Having Your Own Brand: Stand out so everyone wants to work with you

The business world is leaning more toward mass production and brand control, to the point where creating your own innovative product with added value and an open platform is vital. It is important that you expand yourself to not just represent another company's brand, but also work hard to form your own unique identity and brand that others want to associate with. No doubt consolidation is a double-edged sword.

At one point or another into the late 1950s, our family business was involved with Michelin Tires, Mann Trucks, the Roxy and Empire Cinemas among other things. All of those are gone today, but the lesson learned was in how to brand ourselves—how to create added value if we applied our efforts to our own products in parallel to carrying other brands, creating the balance of emphasizing what we had and concurrently seeking new horizons. There's something to be said about going upstream by making your own brand, or even going from service to manufacturing. You can increase the impact on value it could have. With our family business, we built a name associated with quality, dependability, reliability, trust, and honesty.

Just look at the story of Lamborghini S.p.A., which began as a tractor company in northern Italy just after World War II.[29] Founder Ferruccio Lamborghini had made a name for himself building tractors from used military vehicles. As his success grew, Ferruccio indulged his love of fine cars by purchasing Alfa Romeos, Lancias, and Maseratis.

---

29   "Lamborghini Cars Were A Result Of A Tractor Company Owner Being Insulted By The Founder Of Ferrari." *Today I Found Out.* March 2011. www.todayifoundout.com/index.php/2011/03 / lamborghini-cars-were-a -result-of-a-tractor-company-owners-frustration-with-ferrari/

Then, in 1958, Ferruccio purchased his first Ferrari, a 250GT coupe … and was rather disappointed. He bought a few other Ferraris after that but found that he was constantly frustrated with the clutch on all of them.

In a 1991 interview with *Thoroughbred & Classic Cars* magazine, Lamborghini explained:

"All my Ferraris had clutch problems. When you drove normally, everything was fine. But when you were going hard, the clutch would slip under acceleration; it just wasn't up to the job. … The problem with the clutch was never cured, so I decided to talk to Enzo Ferrari. I had to wait for him a very long time. 'Ferrari, your cars are rubbish!' I complained. Il Commendatore was furious. 'Lamborghini, you may be able to drive a tractor but you will never be able to handle a Ferrari properly.' This was the point when I finally decided to make a perfect car."[30]

Lamborghini had an amazing entrepreneurial mind-set, and instead of fiddling around with Ferrari's cars to make them better, he turned his efforts toward making his own vehicle—his idea of the perfect car, with his own name as the brand, proudly bearing the Zodiac symbol of his birth: the bull.

When you create your own brand, you create something that has the potential to grow through multiple generations. You control it, you create the formula behind it, and, ultimately, you can dispense with it as you wish. The world becomes your oyster.

Processes: Creating a unique process contributes to success of a brand

Whether you create your own brand or work within someone else's, the value of creating a unique process that contributes to the success of that brand is practically immeasurable, especially when such care and continuous improvements are placed on the process, making it

---

30 www.400gt.com/articles/compare/interview.htm

difficult if not impossible for others to keep pace with the amassed knowledge as it reaches an exponential state.

One of the greatest examples of an added value process in existence today is Li & Fung, the largest export trading company in Hong Kong.[31]

Founded in 1906 by former English teacher Fung Pak-Liu and Li To-Ming, the business originated when Fung began serving as a buyer's agent between American merchants who didn't speak a bit of Chinese and Chinese factories that didn't speak English.

Fung's fluency in Chinese and English was a valued commodity at the turn of the century, but as travel became more efficient and the gap between buyer and factory began to narrow, Li & Fung's services as buyer's agents were needed less and less.

In 1976, it fell on third-generation Fung family members Victor and William to revitalize the family business, overcome the IE, and bring it to practically unimagined heights, and that's exactly what they did.

In an interview with *Harvard Business Review*, Victor explained how they began by extending their geographic reach, acting as regional sourcing agents and managing the complexities of world trade so that purchasers could go to a single source—Li & Fung—instead of to multiple factories in multiple countries.

They also refined their knowledge of international products so that they could provide the best quality goods from the entire region. For instance, Victor noted that when it came to textiles, synthetics were better in Taiwan but cottons were better in Hong Kong. So, instead of individual companies having to first learn the difference

---

31   Joan Magretta, "Fast, Global, and Entrepreneurial: Supply Chain Management, Hong Kong Style," *Harvard Business Review*, Sept–Oct 1998, https://hbr.org/1998/09/fast-global-and-entrepreneurial -supply-chain-management-hong-kong-style

and then knowledgeably source materials from different factories and regions, Li & Fung handled all of it.

"By working with a larger number of countries, we were able to assemble components; we call this 'assortment packing,'" said Victor. "Say I sell a tool kit to a major discount chain. I could buy the spanners from one country and the screwdrivers from another and put together a product package."[32]

From there, Li & Fung once again switched their entire manufacturing model. Instead of buyers coming to their company and asking them for the best place to buy the product they wanted, Li & Fung became a manager and deliverer of manufacturing items.

For instance, if a clothing company were interested in a new look for next year's fall season, they could go to Li & Fung and say, "This is the style, this is the color, and this is how much we need. What's the best way to produce this?"

Li & Fung would then find the material, find the dye, match the colors, manufacture the garment, create prototypes, and then refine the product until it met the buyer's approval. From there, Li & Fung would take care of the planning and production, ensuring quality and prompt delivery.

That was just the 1980s.

In the early 1990s, Li & Fung developed the breakthrough concept of "dispersed manufacturing."[33] If it cost less for the labor-intensive part of a manufacturing process to be completed in China, for instance, and the actual materials to be created in Taiwan, and for the packaging to be done by Pakistani factories owned by a company

---

32   Ibid.

33   Fu-Lai Tony Yu, Diana S. Kwan, *Chinese Entrepreneurship: An Austrian Economics Perspective* (New York: Routledge, 2016). https://books.google.com/books?id=nDE-CgAAQBAJ&lpg=PT115&dq=fung percent20most percent20studied percent20case percent-20study percent20harvard&pg=PT19#v=onepage&q=fung percent20most percent20studied percent20case percent20study percent20harvard&f=false

in India, and all of that came out to a far better price for the buyer than having the product created all in one place, then Li & Fung managed that process, as well.

From Innovation to Disruptive Change

Because of this model, Li & Fung's annual sales as of May 2017 were $16.76 billion, with the company's market cap at $3.6 billion.[34]

Li & Fung's process has become an added value for businesses on a global scale, and it is something that no other single business can replicate effectively. Li & Fung have perfected their process—they've tapped into a unique angle of international trade.

As a process guy (just like my friend Michel Fatal), I believe that the best way to retain knowledge and cultivate the potential of the people in your organization is to add value, important value, and create processes (as discussed in Chapter 5) to facilitate transparency and increase fluidity based on what they're doing, and improve those processes over the course of time. For multigenerational family businesses, it is a way not only to add value over time, but to shape the present to benefit the future.

Assets, however, are most obvious in their tangible forms, such as real estate, processes, and funds. But just as important to your family business's success are those intangible assets, such as trust, self-worth, and strong communication. And just as with tangible assets, these intangibles can also be passed on from generation to generation.

---

34   Forbes, "The World's Biggest Public Companies" May 2017, www.forbes.com/companies/li-fung/

Intangible Assets

The intangibles, while difficult to quantify, are just as valuable when running and growing a family business. From family values to the value of a high self-worth, intangible assets likely number in the hundreds and vary from business to business, and from person to person. There are certainly more than those I am about to touch on in this chapter, but the following represent a handful of assets that have been of particular significance to the survival of our family business, our family as a whole, and the family businesses examined throughout the book.

Self-Worth: Recognizing your worth is an asset

Recognizing your own self-worth is an asset that should be passed on from one generation to the next. Understanding your own great value and your ability to contribute to the family business is not egotistical—it is invaluable, as is knowing your limits and dismantling them. In understanding your self-worth, you give yourself and your family the strength to best position yourselves in what is often a brutal battlefield of business, and it helps you to unflinchingly hold your ground. Like my friend Mohammed Mohebi once said, "Business is like a puzzle. Every day you get up and strategize on how to make the pieces fit."

Even today, when you go to my great-grandfather's hometown, his name is still recognized because of how bold, strong-willed, and tough he was. Self-confidence is an incredibly important asset when it comes to standing up for what you believe in—and having the stamina to stand—along with sensible business acumen.

As A. H. Baassiri exemplified, if you believe in yourself and your ability to draw yourself out of a difficult situation, then that sense of self-worth can be your savior. It is when you lose this sense, when you buckle to self-doubt, that you lose your bearing.

That said, however, you shouldn't have blind belief in yourself. Rather, you should be open to the evolution of your personality. You should be able to communicate, be able to motivate, and be able to inspire the people around you—give people the confidence to believe in you so that when you need those people most, they will step up and help you turn your dreams into reality. As leadership speaker Simon Sinek says, "People don't buy *what* you do; they buy *why* you do it."[35, 36]

Mark Lee of the family business Sing Lun Holdings is a prime example of having confidence in your own self-worth and decision-making abilities.[37] After several years working outside of his family business in an internationally known technology firm, Mark returned to his family's apparel manufacturing company with an eye to overhauling and the self-confidence to make powerful changes to the company.

It wasn't that the company was doing poorly—the annual turnover was around $48 million in 1999—but after evaluating the company's strengths and banking on the potentials of the sportswear niche market, Mark had quadrupled the company's turnover to $235 million by 2015.

"One thing I've learned is that you have to drive change fearlessly if you're going to continue to grow," said Mark in an interview with PWC.[38] "Not doing this is the single biggest barrier to success—you

---

35   Simon Sinek, "Start with the Why: How Great Leaders Inspire Everyone to Take Action", *Good Reads*, www.goodreads.com/quotes/668292-people-don-t-buy-what-you-do-they-buy-why-you

36   This principle is shared by a forum buddy of mine, M. Moheb.

37   *Great Expectations*, 13.

38   Ibid.

cannot meet the needs of an evolving market if you're not prepared to evolve yourself."

Some years ago, I had to step away from my role in our family business for nearly a year. The move was unplanned and happened literally overnight. I did not expect to stay as long as I did, but when my family and I returned, I found that the company had stepped up brilliantly in my absence. I had left in the middle of a worldwide financial crisis, but it seems all the pre-planning and structure put in place over time had great results. My confidence in the team's skills were well placed, and I found that the company, in fact, had done even better in my absence than when I was around, according to my right-hand person—so much so that I had to seek a new role where I found my passion without stifling the world and confidence of others. I thank family, colleagues, and friends who stepped up during that time. I am also grateful for the new bonds that I made along that journey including KC Chami.

Belief in yourself and belief in your talents and skills are some of the biggest assets you carry with you, though they should always be tapered by the understanding that you ultimately are not as vital and important to your company as you may think—especially if you have done a good job of training your team members and bringing on people who are capable, loyal, and trustworthy. It's your duty to seek talent that actively complements the culture you are striving to build, with the aim of allowing the people, systems, and processes that are collectively put in place to one day replace you, always injecting young blood into the mix, so that you can go on to build more dreams. Such behavior, in my opinion, should always be rewarded.

For business leaders and successful entrepreneurs, a strong sense of self-worth may seem egotistical, but success is not something easily achieved by the weak and malleable. It is the bold, strong-willed, tough individuals who truly institute change, and a team of motivated leaders along your side can do wonders.

In our family business, for instance, each board member and team member brings something unique to the table and completes the puzzle. The ability to allow and organize such talents is key.

Diversification: Seeing beyond your own borders

Traveling, seeing the world, and seeking new challenges are some of the most important ways you can evolve as a person and as a business leader because these actions force you to see the world through the eyes of new and often drastically different views, cultures, and innovations. Starting with my great-grandfather, my father Abdul, and, I hope, our generation, those who follow will continue to seek insight through immersing ourselves in the new and unknown and will continue to be open to moving where the wind blows us. My ancestors were willing to see the opportunities and go where they led, interjecting themselves into whatever societies they wound up in across the globe, even going as far as Asia and North America, learning from the culture and growing their businesses within them. This generation, too, as well as the new one coming up, continues to travel. In fact, my brother Sam, an avid pilot and citizen of the world, has been to more than 175 countries, on many occasions piloting himself to his destinations, and strives to complete visiting every country in the world in the near future. His passion for travel stems from his desire to discover, to see the other view, to seek change.

You must have a global view if you are going to thrive as a global citizen.

Take the Rothschild family, for instance.[39] Mayer Amschel Rothschild, a banker, founded the House of Rothschild in the 1760s when he built a financial house spread across the five main European financial centers of the world: London, Paris, Vienna, Naples, and Frankfurt. To each of these centers he assigned one of his five sons and created a system whereby each son reported what he learned regarding his particular city, sharing that financial and cultural knowledge with all the other sons so that they could learn from it.

If Mayer Rothschild hadn't realized this as an interruption in his business and diversified in the way he had—if he had kept his business solely in his home city of Frankfurt—then it is likely that his business would never have survived World War II. Instead, he scattered his sons—his human assets—across the modern world so that they could not only have the benefit of geographic diversification should one or more of the businesses fail but also the benefit of learning from that culture and region, expanding on their combined intellectual asset.

I don't need to tell you that this plan worked out well for the Rothschild family. Today, the family possesses the largest private fortune in the world, and their interests span from real estate to farming to wine and charities.[40]

Many years ago, my maternal great-grandfather was a nobleman who ruled an area bordering the Levant area in the Middle East. Like the Rothschilds, he worked to strengthen his power and reach by placing each of his kids in different cities and regions so that he could secure and wield his power more effectively.

---

39   Paul Vallely, "The Rothschild Story: A Golden Era Ends for a Secretive Dynasty," *The Independent*, April 16, 2004. https://web.archive.org/web/20060115031554/http://news.independent.co.uk/uk/this_britain/article56239.ece

40   https://en.wikipedia.org/wiki/Rothschild_family

Taking a global view both with your business and your own mind-set may allow you to evolve with your own view. It may even solidify your point of view from a different cultural perspective, but ultimately, it gives you an all-too-important diversified mindset, which in-and-of-itself is an asset.

This global perspective also gives you further confidence in yourself. If you're able to see a problem not just from your own culturally inherent angles but from a point of view informed by the cultural dispositions of nations around the world, it gives you an invaluable belief in yourself and the confidence to implement ideas rather than just dream them. And for that I am thankful to my family, as well as to each and every person who is a part of my forum, all of whom have supported me on my journey to explore, share, and evolve as a person, including this book. My forums are an integral part to my life; part of a group known as the Young Presidents Organization, or YPO.

The Young Presidents Organization (YPO) is a global chief executive leadership organization that I have been a member of for two decades, and over the years it has provided me with numerous useful and diverse cultural perspectives. It has been a safe haven for me to discuss challenges and interruptions with others of equal minds, allowing me to interact with as many as thirty-plus people in different forums who serve as my pseudo-board advisors and who are always available to me, as I am to them. My view is to always have an alternative view, and forum has been an excellent resource for that, providing me with regular opportunities to learn and share and grow.

These shared insights, too, have not only helped me grow my contribution to our family business's worldwide perspective, but it has also helped me grow and evolve as a person. Try and seek such connection around you, be it through forums or elsewhere.

Perception: Keeping balance and an open mind

Two days before my father passed, we were having our weekly family lunch. Dad was the picture of health. We were talking about this and that, a little about business, but mostly about life. To be honest, I was trying my best to talk about business, but that wasn't something my father subscribed to. "There's a time and place for everything," he would say and made it a point to separate family time from work. Because of this, I seek to work hard and play smart with purpose ("seek" being the operative word).

Then, at some point during lunch, my daughters began talking about an acquaintance of theirs.

It wasn't the most rosy of conversations, and on overhearing them, my father paused and got their attention. Now, my father was not an easily forgettable person. He had presence. When he walked in to a room, people noticed; and when he wanted my girls' attention, he had it in an instant.

He proceeded to say, "Don't forget this: Never judge a book by its cover. Flip through the pages, because there's always something more to discover."

The whole time he was saying this, he was gently squeezing my hand in his, as though he knew these words were just as important for me to hear as it was for my daughters. It was, in a way, his last will and testament of advice to me, and he followed it up with one more piece of advice to all of us.

"Hold things in the middle," he said. "On one end, be passionate and compassionate. On the other, be smart and wise."

It is your perception that allows you to evolve. You must take a pause and assess, do away with your mental blocks, your prejudices, the no-can-do attitude, and check yourself again and again, looking at what you're doing. Whenever we're open to change, willing to perceive ourselves as imperfect and yet capable of becoming more, then we become better not only at running a business but better as human beings.

Many of today's most well-known family businesses have survived by keeping an open mind. Take Walmart, for instance—a family business now considered to be one of the largest—if not *the* largest—family business in the world.[41]

Started in 1950, founder Sam Walton hit on the idea of lowering profit margins with the goal of driving more sales and increasing overall profit. The idea took off like wildfire, and by 1975, he had 125 stores in nine states.[42]

Walton could have left it at that, opening more stores in more states and sticking to that one successful concept, but he didn't. Just three years later, the company branched out into pharmaceutical, jewelry, and auto service divisions, and ten years after that, their new Supercenters featured additional services, such as a vision center, photo-processing lab, portrait studio, and basic auto center, as well as alcove shops with banks, salons, fast food restaurants, cell phone companies, and other independent, complementary stores.

With roughly 2.2 million employees and more than $482 billion in revenue as of 2015, Walmart is a family business that has profited enormously from keeping an open mind and an ear to the ground when it comes to opportunities.

Then there is the story behind the near-collapse of Bavarian Motor Works, a German automotive manufacturing company more widely known as BMW. In 1959, BMW was close to either declaring bankruptcy or selling to auto manufacturer Daimler-Benz when Herbert Quandt, a 30 percent shareholder at the time, saw something

---

41   "Top 25 Largest Family-Owned Companies in the World." *Forbes Lists*. www.forbes.com/pictures/geim45eggj/1-wal-mart/#1e28fc5c3673

42   "The History of Walmart," *Wikipedia*, https://en.wikipedia.org/wiki/History_of_Walmart

more in the company. With a new line of unique vehicles just about to hit the assembly line, Quandt believed BMW could succeed. So with an open mind—and most of his family's fortune—he stepped in and gained a controlling interest in the company. The risk paid off when BMW's subsequently released Neue Klasse (New Class) line brought the automaker back from the edge of extinction and to its status as one of the largest family-owned companies in the world.

It was a huge risk and a significant IE, but Quandt saw past the cover of a quickly failing automotive company, choosing instead to flip through the pages and discovering a dynamic and innovative business that he could believe and invest in.

Your Family's Intellectual Capital

When it comes down to it, your family bond is your greatest asset—a fact that is as true in life as it is in your family business. And the most important asset your family brings to the family business table is their intellectual capital.

Regardless of whether their education is through higher learning or life experiences, that wealth of information is a reservoir from which the family can draw to help overcome those IEs that are inevitable in every business cycle.

The trick is to tap into this potential and not take it for granted. Sometimes this can be precarious, as you bring into the boardroom the family dynamics and baggage that you might have grown up with. Family knows how to press each other's buttons (double-edged sword) and you might have no limits with each other. The trick is to nurture the best and drop the rest.

You might also fall into having a sibling relationship while in the boardroom. This is dangerous. You need to know which hat to put on at what time. It's a sensitive balance and one that requires a lot of emotional intelligence.

Great-grandfather A. H. Baassiri was able to learn and grow through the ups and downs of each business cycle, building here, expanding there, and selling off when necessary. With each cycle, he learned a new way to build, developed a new process to follow, and found new ways to survive.

My father's generation took the route of higher education, and the knowledge that he gained has helped the family business at countless important junctures over the years.

I speak about education in Chapter 6, but as an asset, I and many other family businesses today hold the intellectual capital of our family members, gained through both experience and education, in the highest regard.

According to a study published in the *International Entrepreneurship and Management Journal*, "The current trend is for organizations to focus less on material assets and more on intangible assets when seeking competitive advantages and that those firms with adequate intellectual capital have a better chance of survival."[43]

Ramon Mendiola, for instance, was able to use his well-earned intellectual capital from working for multinational companies Kraft Foods and Philip Morris when he came back to Costa Rica to head up the family business, Florida Ice and Farm Company (FIFCO).

"When I joined [FIFCO], I tried to take the best out of the multinationals [such as accountability], but at the same time also

---

43   Esther Horminga, Rosa M. Batista-Canino, Agustin Sancehs-Mendina, "The Role of Intellectual Capital in the Success of New Ventures," *International Entrepreneurship and Management Journal* 2010, www.ub.edu/greie/estils/pdf/the_role_of_intellectual_capital_in_the_succes_of_new_ventures.pdf

to keep some of those family-related values that for me were quite important," said Mendiola.[44]

In taking what he learned and turning it to focus more toward family values, such as treating people as more than "just a number" and cutting down on unnecessary bureaucracy, he was able to blend both family and nonfamily business perspectives in a way that has greatly benefited the structure of the publicly traded Costa Rican company.

Passion: Find joy in what you do

Anything you do that turns into a business, no matter how much you love it, is going to become work; you will last longer if you love it, but you're not going to enjoy it all of the time. The same holds true across every profession, no matter how fun the job may seem. Acting, for instance, can be a brutal career: filming at three in the morning, hours of makeup, months spent away from family, unending social obligations, and utter lack of privacy are only a handful of the downsides, and I'm sure any actor could list a hundred more.

There is nothing wrong with having a cocktail of wishes. Find something around you to dream about. Find something you love in what you already do, and be adamant about balancing work and play. In family business, this is an incredibly important asset. While you may not love every aspect of what you do, it is likely that there's some part of the business that speaks to your passions. And if there isn't, you might be able to create it and ultimately improve the business because of it.

I learned this lesson fifteen years after I started working for our family business. One day, I just found myself looking around the

---

44   "Are Family Businesses the Best Model for Emerging Markets?" *Wharton University of Pennsylvania*, May 31, 2016, http://knowledge.wharton.upenn.edu/article/family-business-model-works-better-markets-others/

office, evaluating my position, and thinking, "You know what? I don't think I love what I do."

It wasn't that I planned to leave the family business, but I was at a crossroad. I was either going to reach a point of feeling unsatisfied, or I had to abridge my attitude and find something I loved about my job.

That thought stuck with me for months until one day, after voicing my concern for the hundredth time at one of my forums, my forum buddy, Ziad Makkawi, turned to me and said, "What is it that you want to do?"

Everything stopped. I had been complaining about what I *didn't* want for so long, and yet I hadn't thought about what I *did* want.

Without thinking, I just said the first thing that came to mind.

"I want to play the guitar," I told him.

"So play the guitar," he replied. "Who's stopping you from learning?"

"Nobody."

"Then play the guitar."

It took me another eight years from that moment to sign up for a guitar lesson and actually get a guitar, and even then it wasn't a guitar I bought for me—it was my daughter's old guitar, which I had restrung so I could play it left-handed. This was triggered by my close pal Craig Enenstein, who inspired me to actually start taking guitar lessons when I learned at one of my father-daughter camps that he himself took up playing the guitar with his daughter, Whitney, as a means to create a common bond. I took lessons for a year and planned to play the song "Father and Son" by Cat Stevens for my father.

Unfortunately, I never had a chance to play it for him. I rehearsed it to my dear friend, Basel Hamwi, the night before my dad unexpectedly passed away.

Guitar playing, of course, isn't a part of our family business. I found something else to love within that. But finding a passion that was just for me, that was outside of work, was rewarding in and of itself, and it helped me to elaborate on the lesson "Find what you love in what you do." For instance, writing is another passion of mine, and here I am, making it happen!

Many of us complain every day about what we don't like about our jobs, but few of us take the time to look on the other side of the coin and ask, "But what *do* I like?"

This has helped me find more to like in what I do at my job, and for me, my happiness turned out to be in processes and systems.

When it comes to processes, I don't believe that you always have to be reinventing the wheel. If a process already exists, study it. That is, if someone tells me, "This is hot," I don't put my finger on it just to make sure they're right. I see it is red. I see it is emanating heat waves. I don't need to take that extra step and burn myself. I learn from their experience.

This is an approach that was part nature and part nurture for me growing up. As a kid, I was always an observer—a habit that was nurtured by the fact that I was almost always the youngest in my class. If older kids already knew how to ride a bike, I watched and learned from the summary of their mistakes and used that as a baseline in order to save myself time.

That habit eventually turned into a love of processes. I innately understood that I didn't have to start every day by repeating the same inefficient habits. Instead, I could develop procedures that made results quicker, clearer, and more effective.

For instance, I know that my drawer for my socks is going to be closest to my shoes because there's no point in going back and forth between shoes and socks. And my smartphone and iPad will always be closest to the door because I'll need those things as I'm leaving home for the day. My work related items will be in place, for the same reasons. Someday, technology will advance to the point where a chip under our skin replaces our smartphones, iPads, and I wonder what else! Hopefully making our to-do lists shorter, and increasing the time we have to sit and reflect.

It is about reviewing the process to build in efficiencies, and when you build in efficiencies, you are also gathering knowledge in one place so that it becomes an asset. By getting from A to B in the fastest way, and reviewing processes to constantly improve on them, you're able to break things down to their first principle, rebuilding on them so that, ultimately, you waste even less time.

No one lives forever, so what you make with the time you have can become a great advantage. That said, I have learned that molding time to one's advantage doesn't necessarily mean that I'm shrinking time. Instead, I'm affording myself the opportunity to start on a project earlier than others would start on it, or to start at the same time but finish sooner, because I've already learned from past mistakes.

We all have things that frustrate us as individuals. For me, my frustration comes from people repeating, without seeking to improve upon, something that has been formalized and standardized, because they've "stuck to just the rule book" and decided not to take into account all possibilities. But you should review, you should learn from the past and present while anticipating the future.

There's a serenity to processes that brings me joy, and I've been able to help the company in many ways because of it.

I found my niche, and when I get to do it, I do it with passion.

The son of one of the richest men in America did the same thing in finding his niche and following it, and his father was wise to let him follow his own path because it ultimately benefited the long-term preservation of the family's wealth.

John D. Rockefeller only had one son, his namesake, John D. Rockefeller Jr. In his lifetime, the senior Rockefeller had famously accumulated wealth that, at its peak, was equal to 2 percent of the American economy, making him one of the richest people in modern history, if not *the* richest.[45] But when his son expressed no interest in a business career, Rockefeller Sr. didn't contradict him.

Instead of following in his father's footsteps, John D. Rockefeller Jr. pursued a career in philanthropy and careful investments, such as financing the Rockefeller Center in New York City and donating the land for the site of the Museum of Modern Art.[46]

For his own family, however, Junior set up a familiar system: a wealth-management office for family members geared toward building on the family's intellectual and human capital. Through it, his six children—five sons and a daughter—had the means to pursue careers that spoke to their passions and, consequently, allowed them to make significant contributions in philanthropy, politics, conservation, and banking.[47]

There is something to love in everything in this world, even the ugliest, dirtiest jobs. And when you find that small joy, you can build on it, slowly at first and then more and more, until you can bring it into balance with the rest of your job. But finding that happiness and developing it depends on you.

---

45   "The Richest Americans in History" *CNN*, June 2, 2014, http://money.cnn.com/gallery/luxury/2014/06/01/richest-americans-in-history/

46   https://en.wikipedia.org/wiki/John_D._Rockefeller_Jr.

47   https://en.wikipedia.org/wiki/John_D._Rockefeller_III

If there's truly nothing at all that speaks to your passion, however, then first ask yourself what you *do* want. Once you know what that is, consider that somehow that passion could benefit your family's business as much as it does you. You may surprise yourself.

Communication: Businesses split because of poor communication

For as long as I can remember, my father told me, "You have two eyes, two ears, and one mouth, so you have to observe and listen more."

The ability to openly communicate and resolve conflict amicably within a range of situations, including a family business, is vital. Business after family business has split because of a poor communication.

Take the Gucci family, for instance.

A series of lawsuits between second-generation business leader Aldo Gucci and his son Paolo caused a severe rift in the family, and accusations that Aldo's nephew and successor as chairman of Gucci, Maurizio, had forged key documents only deepened the divide.[48]

After all was said and done, nearly 50 percent of the interest in Guccio Gucci S.p.A. was sold to an undisclosed investment banking firm in the Middle East in 1988, all because of the fierce fighting between family members.

The Guccis' feud, however, is certainly on the extreme end of poor family communication and insufficient conflict management. For the majority of family companies, a joint EY/Kennesaw State University survey evaluating lasting success in family business found that only about 21 percent state that they are often engaged in dys-

---

48   Isadore Barmash, "Gucci Family, Split by Feud, Sells Large Stake in Retailer," *New York Times*, June 8, 1988, www.nytimes.com/1988/06/08/business/gucci-family-split-by-feud-sells-large-stake-in-retailer.html

functional conflicts, and a healthy 84 percent say that they are proud of being a part of the family.[49]

Conflict is inevitable, no matter how well your family gets along or how well your family constitution is written. It is how your family handles it and how well they work through the interruption that speaks to the strength of your family's unity and trust in each other. Each voice must have a means to be heard. Fortunately, even as family businesses spread, with many reaching across countries and continents, the ability to communicate has gotten easier. In fact, the survey noted above goes on to state that 43 percent of respondents used social media, including family intranet and face-to-face technology, for business-related communication.

Apart from electronic communication, the survey adds that family communication is facilitated by regular family meetings, with 90 percent of participants stating that they have regular family or shareholder meetings focused on business, while 70 percent have regular meetings just for family issues, and 64 percent have a family council that meets regularly. We are keen on this in our family, as well.

Flexibility: Be able to learn and adjust to new situations

Another instrumental intangible asset is the ability to learn from and adjust to new situations. For me, that asset has manifested in learning to be flexible about things like working in the grease-covered trenches of the service parts industry to learn about just one aspect of our family business, all the way to jumping on airplanes and giving presentations at the drop of a hat. It even provided me with the

---

49   "Staying Power: How Do Family Businesses Create Lasting Success? Global Survey of the World's Largest Family Businesses," *EY.com*, 2015. www.ey.com/Publication/vwLUAssets/ey-staying-power-how-do-family-businesses-create-lasting-success/$FILE/ey-staying-power-how-do-family-businesses-create-lasting-success.pdf

opportunity to learn a new language, though I didn't see it as much of an opportunity at the time.

On this occasion, my father had sent me to a board meeting in Germany. I got there, sat down, and the board meeting began. In German.

Note, one unique quality about my family is how well many of us can learn and retain new languages. Between my siblings and me, we can speak a number of languages, following in the footsteps of my maternal grandfather, who published in several languages.

However, I didn't speak a word of German, and I sat through that whole board meeting unable to understand a thing. When I left, all I could think was, "How can I understand and integrate all this?"

But I wasn't going to let a little language barrier keep me from doing my job. Right after that meeting, I found a language education center and took twenty-six hours of German. When the second board meeting came around, I walked in, sat down, heard everything they said in German, understood some of it, and wrote down questions as we went along. Then I turned around and spoke my questions to them in broken German.

They were blown away, as I hoped. My intention had been to adjust to their way of doing things. But in taking the time to learn their language—if even on a very basic level—I'd shown them that I was willing to do what was needed to make our partnership succeed. I gained their respect for the duration of that partnership—it was *sehr gut!*[50]

First-generation business owner Angela Romero faced a similar interruption when she moved to the United States from Cali, Columbia, in 1997.

---

50   Translation from German: Really good!

Knowing very little English, Angela began a small business selling clothing out of a suitcase to fellow business administration students. Over the years, however, she was able to overcome the challenge of learning a new language, and by 2016, her company was ranked as one of the top 500 fastest-growing companies in the United States.

According to an article in *Inc. 5000*, Angela "faced a language barrier, in addition to prejudice—from mostly male suppliers who initially refused to speak with her because she is a female who speaks with an accent."[51]

But this didn't hold Angela back. "At the beginning, I was shy and afraid to speak to my suppliers because of my English," she explained. But that was before she realized, "I don't need to be perfect with my language skills; I just need to be able to communicate and get what I need."[52]

It was this confidence—and her burgeoning bilingual skills— that bolstered her as she built her business from that one-person mobile shop to a 17,000-square-foot warehouse with a 2015 revenue of $4.4 million and an international clientele.

Even if you've never left your own country, learning other languages and studying new cultures can prove to be the stepping stones your family business needs to reach the next level. "Learning a new language or culture in the business world has tremendous value in a global marketplace," said Victoria Berry, program manager of Business and Performance Development with Corporate College, in an article for Smart Business Network. "Even within your own

---

51   Kerry Close, "Top Latino Entrepreneurs Recount Trials and Triumphs of Starting Up in the U.S." *Inc 5000*, www.inc.com/kerry-close/top-latino-entrepreneurs-cite-background-as-asset.html

52   Etelka Lehoczky, "From Selling Clothes Out of a Suitcase to Running a $4.2 Million Company," *Inc 5000*, www.inc.com/kerry-close/top-latino-entrepreneurs-cite-background-as-asset.html

company, you can have people from different cultures working together on high-functioning and cross-functional teams."[53]

If you're looking to expand your market globally, Berry points out, "On top of the more visible language barrier, cultural misunderstandings can be just as dangerous. . . . For instance, in China, it's considered discourteous to take someone's business card and not look at it, or at least pretend to read the title. As another example, you wouldn't want to call a Mexican company between noon and three p.m. when businesses are closed, or discuss business during lunchtime."

In fact, 20 percent of global family businesses surveyed by PricewaterhouseCoopers (PWC) in 2012 listed "understanding business cultures overseas" as one of the main challenges to conducting international business.[54]

Flexibility and adapting to new situations, however, are some of the main qualities that define a successful family business.

When faced with an unknown language, a foreign culture, and no credit history, Asam Mujili arrived in the United States from Iraq with some difficult barriers to overcome.[55] But six years later, he became the proud owner of family-operated Ishtar Market and Restaurant in Idaho, where his traditional Arabic food has been celebrated for its "consistently good meals" and its "large loaves of flatbread baked in-house [that] have been a hit."[56]

53   Jayne Gest, "How Learning a New Language and Culture Can Be Valuable in the Business World," *Smart Business*, Aug 1, 2012, www.sbnonline.com/article/ how-learning-a-new-language-and-culture-can-be-valuable-in-the-business-world-corpcollege/

54   "The Family Firm: Central to the Success of the Middle East," *PwC Family Business Survey* 2012, www.pwc.com/m1/en/publications/documents/family-firm-english.pdf

55   Marcia Drew Hohn, "Immigrant Entrepreneurs: Creating Jobs and Strengthening the Economy." *Immigrant Learning Center (ILC) Public Education Institute*, Jan 2012. www.uschamber.com/ sites/default/files/legacy/reports/Immigrant percent20Entrepreneur percent20final percent201-22-2012.pdf

56   Rachel Daigle, "Ishtar Market and Restaurant: Restaurants You Should Know About," *Boise Weekly*, March 15, 2011. www.boiseweekly.com/boise/ishtar-market-and-restaurant/ Content?oid=2121109

In Massachusetts, immigrants founded more than 60 percent of new business just in 2008, despite only making up 14 percent of the state's population. According to the US Census Bureau, "These entrepreneurs have aided economic recovering by fostering commerce, innovation, and job growth."[57]

Family Values: These can be an ethical driving force of a family business

The first year after my father passed away, I found myself competing with a giant.

"What did my mentor do in his lifetime? How can I continue to evolve and learn and grow as he did?" I asked myself and then tried to do what I thought he would have done.

But as much as any of us may try, we can't compete with the heroes of the past. What I concluded was that I could live by our family values and allow those values to be the ethical driving force behind how I conduct myself and how we run our businesses as a family.

Let us take as example the 150-year-old family business Cargill, for whom those family values are a vital part of their corporate philosophy and reflect the responsibility they feel toward "help[ing to] meet complex economic, environmental, and social challenges wherever we do business." These not only include their four main commitments of food security (a term Cargill describes as "nourishing the world's growing population while at the same time protecting the planet"), food safety leadership, responsible supply chains, and environmental sustainability, but also the company's Guiding Principles:

- We obey the law

---

57   Marcia Drew Hohn, "Immigrant Entrepreneurs: Creating Jobs and Strengthening the Economy." *Immigrant Learning Center (ILC) Public Education Institute*, Jan 2012

- We conduct our business with integrity

- We keep accurate and honest records

- We honor our business obligations

- We treat people with dignity and respect

- We protect Cargill's information, assets, and interests

- We are committed to being a responsible global citizen

"Since 1865, when W.W. Cargill founded our company, Cargill has acted on the belief that doing the right thing sets the foundation for long-term success," Cargill states under its ethics and values. "The Cargill Guiding Principles are the foundation of our vision and articulate our shared ethical values and expectations."[58]

In family business, stating these values loud and clear in your family constitution and living by them every day in your word and deed sets a clear precedent for team members and gives your clients faith in your company.

---

58 www.cargill.com/company/ethics-compliance/index.jsp

CHAPTER 3

Strength in Structure vs. Strength in Fluid Form

"The past has revealed to me the structure of the future."
—PIERRE TEILHARD DE CHARDIN, FRENCH PHILOSOPHER

In 1962, United States president John F. Kennedy gave a speech at the University of California, recognizing the school's 94th anniversary and extolling the value that the school placed on taking "the long view of the shore dimly seen."[59,60]

"We must think and act not only for the moment but for our time," said Kennedy. "I am reminded of the story of the great French Marshal Lyautey, who once asked his gardener to plant a tree. The gardener objected that the tree was slow growing and would not

---

59   President John F. Kennedy, "Address at the University of California at Berkeley, March 23, 1962," https://www.jfklibrary.org/Research/Research-Aids/JFK-Speeches/University-of-California-Berkeley_19620323.aspx

60   JFK also famously paraphrased the words of Lebanese-American author Khalil Gibran in his inaugural address when he said, "Ask not what your country can do for you, but what you can do for your country." In 1923, Gibran had written a similar statement in his article "The New Frontier," which read: "Are you a politician asking *what your country can do for you* or a zealous one *asking what you can do for your country?* If you are the first, then you are a parasite; if the second, then you are an oasis in the desert." www.bartleby.com/73/766.html

reach maturity for one hundred years. The Marshal replied, 'In that case, there is no time to lose! Plant it this afternoon.'"

It is just the same for family businesses. Time should not be measured by days, months, or years, but rather by generations. A common timeframe applied to family business planning is that short term is twenty years, mid term is fifty, and long term is one hundred years.

The dilemma, however, is in balancing business cycles with disruptive changes. Even though a generational cycle may be twenty years, the average life span of an S&P 500 company is shrinking to an average of fifteen years. So, while it is typical to plan to review family constitutions and corporate governance every ten years or so, this shortened life cycle means that the review times should also be shorter—anywhere from every ten years to every three months. In other words, it should be viewed from a zoom in–zoom out perspective—you need to zoom in and plan more frequently for the near future while also zooming out and considering the implications of your planning for generations to come.

Creating a Family Constitution: The Journey

"Ideas are great, but until the people involved are ready to implement them, you're not going to get anywhere."
—SUZY KANOO

The biggest interruption in coming up with a family constitution and corporate governance is this: When it comes to family business, later generations may think that they see exactly what's wrong with the company and how to fix it, but until the matriarch and patriarch agree to it, agree to its implementation and timeline, then nothing is going to happen.

When my parents first proposed creating corporate governance and a family constitution, we all thought it was a great idea. Everyone was enthusiastic—until we commenced with the process.

It was time consuming, tedious, and, in our case, enraging due to the initial third party we selected to helped guide us. However, with the wise, calm, and steady leadership of our parents and the correct advice, we sought a path to achieve a suitable defined structure.

According to the International Finance Corporation, "Because most families run their businesses themselves (at least during the first and second generations), there is usually very little interest in setting clearly articulated business practices and procedures. As the family and its business grow larger, this situation can lead to many inefficiencies and internal conflicts that could threaten the continuity of the business."[61]

The necessity for structure, and particularly one that is fluid, allowing for changes while maintaining a firm foundation, is paramount. The failure to establish any kind of family governance, for instance, impacts many family businesses (as indicated in Chapter 1), particularly in ensuring the succession policy for multiple generations.

One such example of this IE almost collapsed a massive family business in China in 2008.[62]

In December 2008, Huang Guangyu, chairman of China's largest appliance retailer Gome Electrical Appliances Holding Limited, was

---

61   International Finance Corporation, *IFC Family Business Governance Handbook*, 3rd Edition, 2011. www.ifc.org/wps/wcm/connect/6a9001004f9f5979933cff0098cb14b9/FamilyBusinessGovernance_Handbook_English.pdf?MOD=AJPERES

62   Ernesto J. Poza, "Family Governance White Paper – Family Governance: How Leading Families Manage the Challenges of Wealth," *Credit Suisse*, 2012, www.credit-suisse.com/media/pb/docs/sg/privatebanking/services/cs-family-governance-white-paper.pdf

removed from his role following accusations of stock manipulation and was sentenced to fourteen years in prison.

Unfortunately, there was no system of family governance dictating what would happen if Huang was no longer in his role, so once he officially resigned from his position in January 2009, the board of directors and newly appointed chairman faced a significant uphill battle.

In this case, because Huang had relied on his "social capital and high-profile identity" for his continued success, the reputation-ruining accusations of fraud and his subsequent removal as chairman were immediately destructive to the value of his company. In order to right the ship, the board and new chairman fortunately enacted several family governance steps:

- Restructuring of the board of directors to represent the interest of all shareholders, not just the family majority, by appointing three independent nonexecutive directors, three nonexecutive directors, and five executive directors

- Formation of an independent audit committee

- Bringing in of an outside investor with voting rights

- Conducting an internal audit and control review for better transparency on company financials

- Restoration of confidence with key accounts and suppliers, conducted by top management

- Drafting of a five-year strategic plan establishing best management and governance practices

It took two years to recover from Huang's sudden departure, but the turnaround was impressive. However, if Huang had put family governance in place proactively, the crisis could have been averted and the family wealth protected.

Even if you do get everyone on board for putting together family governance and you are able to build your mission, vision, values, and constitution, a lack of trust between family members can quickly ruin everything you've built. Sadly, this is a common issue in family businesses. For example, the family business Vega Food Company was on rocky ground internally for a couple of years because of it.[63]

When the founder of Vega Food Company, Francisco Valle Sr., died suddenly in a car accident, his son, Francisco Valle Jr., was ready to take his role. However, the rest of the family had their doubts. His sisters were concerned about what they felt was his ambitious attitude and tendency toward extravagant tastes.

After a couple of years, Francisco hosted the first family council meeting (a feat on its own). It was held after a full day of meeting with all of the shareholders and discussed the company's present financial situation. He also brought in a family business advisor who spoke with each member of the family before the meeting to discuss their concerns and what they most hoped to gain from the meeting, providing an unbiased voice for the shareholders.

All three of Francisco's sisters expressed at least one concern that had its roots in trust. His youngest sister, Mari, wanted more transparency on the rights of shareholders, whereas Teresa, the middle sister, worried about too much centralization by Francisco and the need for more balance between him and the three sisters. His eldest sister, Isabel, added to Mari's call for clarity, stating, "Things have to be clear for everybody … so that there is no second-guessing later."

---

63   Ibid.

By the end of that first meeting, the family had determined the need for a well-organized family council and a board of directors, as well as the need for clarity and organization.

They had also drafted a basic action plan that included an external valuation of the company that would include a clarified company hierarchy, which all family members agreed to respect. Additionally, they agreed that their board of directors should include independent outsiders and a set list of responsibilities, such as providing oversight on large capital investment decisions and reviewing business strategy, and that shareholders were to be consulted when it came to the selection of board members.

I'd say that was a quick turnaround! For most family businesses, however, it is wise to factor in a longer time frame.

For the Valle family, it was the first step toward reestablishing the trust they had been lacking, and it has proved profitable to the Valle family. Five years after that first meeting, the value of the family enterprise grew five-fold.

In truth, about 60 percent of family wealth disappears because of a lack of communication and trust between family members, according to a survey conducted by a family-wealth consultation company, the Williams Group. And an additional 3 percent of that loss is due to failures in financial planning, taxes, and investments accounts.[64]

I can say that trust in each other as family members certainly proved to be a foundational block after my father's passing and ties us even more than any trust fund could.

---

64   Abby Schultz, "Why Asia's Rich Need a Family Constitution," *Barron's*, Jan 9, 2015. www.barrons.com/articles/why-asias-rich-need-a-family-constitution-1420777286

Framing Your Family Constitution

When you are preparing to write your family governance, or even just talking about the idea to the rest of the family, it is important that you both understand and convey to them that it isn't going to be a perfect document. It is not the word of God. In fact, most family businesses revise their governance minimally every generation, with most revising them every five to ten years, if not more frequently, as mentioned earlier.

Because things change. You have more kids, you get older, the business changes, technology changes, and concepts become outdated. The document can anticipate many things, but it can't see the future, and it can't be so staid and inflexible that it falls apart under the strain of changing situations. It must be fluid—a living, breathing document that allows the system to continue to function smoothly, even as one leader leaves office and another takes that place. It should allow for the solidity and longevity of founding elements such as your company's mission and vision, or its Mass Transformative Purpose—the way in which your company plans to change the world.

The first time I was asked what our family business's main purpose was, I remember saying that it was to "Stay united as a family with a purpose." But the more I thought about it, the more I realized that our purpose isn't just about family; it's more than that. A Mass Transformative Purpose (MTP) speaks to the impact you want to make on a grand scale, and for us, that MTP is "To Give Back"—to be good citizens, contribute to society, and create educational opportunity. That's a more cohesive business purpose. Philanthropy is a noble aim and something we strive for, with the help of the returns of our business and/or other renewable financial means, and we strive to work hard to achieve great things so that we will be able to give back to society.

When it comes to stating an MTP and writing a constitution, one of the most well-known examples in the world is the *United States Constitution*. Within that document is one of the most eloquent MTP's ever stated: ". . . in Order to form a more perfect Union, establish Justice, insure domestic Tranquility, provide for the common defense, promote the general Welfare, and secure the Blessings of Liberty to ourselves and our Posterity. . ."

The document then goes on to address how the Constitution itself can be amended. The Founding Fathers of the United States knew that their Constitution would need to be changed from time to time, but they also knew that it would need to be a carefully thought-out change. So, the article—specifically Article Five of the United States Constitution—makes it difficult, but not impossible, to change fundamental rules. In fact, since the Constitution was enacted in 1789, only twenty-seven amendments have been adopted, ratified by the required number of states, and made a valid part of the Constitution.

Which is why, if you're looking for a model constitution to help you both understand and begin framing out your own family constitution, there are plenty of examples out there, but the US Constitution is a pretty solid paradigm.

First: Start with a mission statement

The mission statement of any constitution is not written just for the present family business construct but for the many generations to come. It is the foundational statement of your family business: your values, your goals, and your expectations for those who will come after you.

"We the people of the United States, in Order to form a more perfect Union, establish Justice, insure domestic Tranquility, provide for the common defense, promote the general Welfare, and secure the Blessings of Liberty to ourselves and our Posterity, do ordain and establish this Constitution for the United States of America."

The Preamble to the Constitution does an excellent job of defining these values, goals, and foundational purpose. It also shows you that a mission statement doesn't need to be a long, drawn-out document—some of the most powerful statements in the world fit into a single sentence.

The mission statement, however, isn't guidance. It defines your intentions, but it doesn't tell future generations *how* you expect to get there. That is where the Articles come in.

Next: Establish governing articles

Just as the Constitution defines the country's governance and how the three branches—executive, legislative, and judicial—should keep each other in balance, so your constitution should clearly establish the responsibilities of each governing body—be it a single family council or a combination of council and board of directors—and the basic operational structure of each, including how leaders are selected and a standard code of conduct. In the United States, if something should happen to the president, for instance, the law of succession passes that power down to the vice president. If not the VP, then the role is passed down to the Senate president pro tempore, then the Speaker of the House, and so on. And when the president's term is over, often a whole new set of representatives comes into place, but the system itself is not affected. It continues uninterrupted.

Also: Include a Bill of Rights

The US Constitution's Bill of Rights was added after objections were raised about the lack of specific guarantees of personal freedoms and rights. Together, these first ten amendments to the Constitution guaranteed those rights, set clear limits on governmental power, and clarified that powers not specifically entrusted to Congress by the Constitution belonged to the states or to the people.

Your Bill of Rights can do the same thing, clarifying the rights of family member—and other—shareholders, as well as defining their basic obligations and responsibilities. When these are clearly established, they can go far in helping to resolve family conflicts, particularly when difficulties arise due to lack of adherence to the accepted family structure, such as when the old sense of entitlement rears its ugly head.

For the Miro family, owners of the Miro Media Group, the creation of a family constitution was integral to the IE of a successful transition between generation three and four.[65] Though the process of creating the constitution and complete secession plans took several years to complete, the end result was not only a smooth transition in family business leadership, but also the establishment of regular family meetings that proved essential in keeping the lines of constructive communication open between family members.

According to a case study on the Miro family conducted by Credit Suisse, one in-law of the Miro family stated, "I am a lot more confident and optimistic since these family meetings started and the brothers and sisters started communicating more and more regularly. It takes time to express and listen to other opinions and understand the different perspectives. Without it … all you are doing is competing."

---

65   Poza, "Family Governance."

EXAMPLE: OUTLINE OF A FAMILY CONSTITUTION

No two family constitutions are the same, but most share similar foundational elements. The mission and objective of the company are basic elements, as well as a family employment policy and the structure of governing bodies. Below is a brief sample outline of a family constitution based on these shared qualities:

Introduction

- Company Purpose/Mission

- Summary of what the family constitution addresses

- How the constitution is approved and how it may be amended

Who We Are

- Family and Company Values that everyone adheres to

Our Ultimate Goals/Who We Want to Be

What you hope the business will ultimately accomplish, both in its given industry as well as internally, in terms of becoming the company you've always envisioned. For example:

- Externally, you hope to become so well-known as a brand that you no longer need to use your name—everyone around the world recognizes your logo (e.g. Starbucks).

- Internally, you want your company to be *the* place for top talent in your field to work because of the top-notch environment, benefits, and reputation.

Our Relationship with Clients

What clients can expect from your company and what you expect from your clients. For example:

- We guarantee the best customer service in the industry
- Our customers are excited about new product launches and are dedicated followers on social media

Our Relationship with Shareholders

- What shareholders can expect from your company. For example:
  - ⌗ We plan to enter twenty-five new markets every five years
  - ⌗ How we plan to facilitate shareholder liquidity

Our Relationship with Vendors

- What vendors can expect from your company. For example:
  - ⌗ 100 percent guarantee on consistent quality

Policy for Employing Family Members

- How family members may enter the family business. Typically, these include rules such as following the same application and approval process as nonmembers, as well as no special privileges, and salary expectations that are the same as nonmembers.

Ownership Expectations and Requirements

- Guidelines on controlling ownership and what principles/responsibilities owners are expected to adhere to, as well their limitations on authority and relationship with the company's governing board(s).

Family Board and Company Board/Board of Directors Expectations and Requirements

- Guidelines for selecting board members, what principles board members should adhere to, responsibilities, relationship with other board members/owners, and limitations on authority

- Guidelines and expectations for meetings

  ◻ Including how often each board should meet and how often the family constitution should be reviewed to ensure the business is following agreed-upon best practices

- Purpose and goal of each board

Guidelines for Conflict Resolution

- How internal problems and conflicts can best be resolved on all levels, from team member to owners

- Guidelines for forming a conflict resolution committee, should one be necessary

---

In our family business, we have created our own documents.

Find a Trustworthy Advisor

When it came to creating our family constitution and corporate governance, we went through the mill with several different advisors, from those working with financial institutions (who, in my experience, tended to carry multiple agendas) to independent consultants.

Each had their positives and negatives, but the most difficult hurdle to overcome was finding an advisor with that essential "human touch" who cared about taking the time to understand not only the family members but also the motivations, connections, and intricacies that make our family what it is—and guiding us as to how those relationships could best be translated on paper. For a number of the advisors we worked with, there was no need or desire for a relationship—it was about the speed and time frame of their deliverables. If we spent more time with them trying to explain our family's interaction with itself, it was just more time for them to bill.

For our family, one of our challenges was that the buy-in was there, but the clarity of the deliverable meant an added frustration when it came to the process of implementation. We were delivering a new baby into the world called Corporate Structure, and every one of our roles was affected by what that document said. We wanted to know it inside and out and have the help we needed to word it just so.

It was often a difficult task getting a clear, detailed explanation from an advisor, although they always had plenty of documents. In the end, our family constitution isn't a perfect document, but no family governance ever will be.

And it was certainly needed. We didn't want a situation where the family business could possibly be lost entirely due to lack of governance. But we later learned the importance and need to share this with our partners as well, so the circle became complete (a topic for another conversation), just as this chapter is meant to share with others.

"We don't have any problems" is a typical statement when family governance is first proposed to family members. "Why do you want to impose a structure on our business that will challenge everything, life and death, who is heir, who will inherit, and what will happen to the in-laws in the business? Why are you creating friction?"

No one wants to deal with the inevitable, because it's easier not to deal with it. But the wise businessperson doesn't look at how they can solve today's problem; they look at how they can solve them tomorrow, next week, and twenty years into the future (which is considered to be the short term by some). You cannot predict the future, but you can put best practices in place today that can help provide agreed-upon guidance when troubles arise.

Family employment

One of the particularly tough topics to broach in any family business is family employment: Should you hire Uncle Arthur or Cousin Chandi just because he or she is family? If you don't have clear parameters in place defining the terms under which family members can be hired, you might find yourself in a very awkward situation, which is why clearly defining this can become a very valuable aspect of your family governance.

My siblings and I all went through training either outside first, or dived into the corporations associated with our family business, which put us in a "corporation mind-set" that we were able to carry into the corporate structure of our family business. But just because we had this training didn't mean that we were afforded any special status. (Well, maybe we were, but at least not to the degree that we saw with the younger generation in other family businesses.) We were expected to earn our places based on merit by learning and proving ourselves along the way. And even if one of us ever needed to step out of the business, that was also factored for as part of the planning we did for our family governance.

A great example of family governance when it comes to family employment can be found in a handbook on Family Business written by the International Finance Corporation in 2011.[66] In it, they call out the case study of the Saad and Bistany families, who founded SABIS.

SABIS has its roots in the village of Choueifat, Lebanon, where the Reverend Tanois Saad and Louisa Proctor started the International School of Choueifat in 1886.[67] The school offers a college-preparatory educational program that grew beyond Lebanon in the

---

66   International Finance Corporation, *IFC Family Business Governance Handbook.*

67   www.sabis.net/educational-services/about/history-services

1970s, eventually expanding into twenty countries on five continents.[68] Today, more than 70,000 students are taught through the SABIS network.

With two families involved, the need to set expectations regarding family employment with the company was clear. In 2006, the SABIS Family Council approved a family employment policy that included not only guidelines on hiring, firing, and educational requirements, but also stated the company's clear philosophy on hiring relations:

"A job at SABIS is neither a birthright nor an obligation for family members. Once hired, family members will be treated as all other non-family employees."

It goes on to state that, "In line with our employment philosophy, the company should not be considered a 'shelter for family members in search of a job,'" and clarifies that any family member who seeks employment with SABIS after the age of forty will have their professional career path evaluated by the board, as well as "the reasons they did not join earlier" before deciding on employment.

Above all, SABIS's policy is clear regarding how family member employees will be treated just like any other non-family employee, from educational prerequisites to training, promotions, grounds for dismissal, and compensation.

However, since the network is so broad and family members will inevitably interact with each other in the workspace, the governance policy goes on to clarify guidelines concerning the hiring of spouses, the avoidance of having family members report to other family members, and the opportunity for young family members to participate in short-term internships.

Our family subscribes to clear family employment guidelines that speak to how we are able to help bring clarity to members of the

---

68   www.sabis.net/

family on how and what is possible. Providing executive cover does not mean covering executive shortfalls.

My own experience in working for our family business early on was eye-opening (see Chapter 6) and exactly what I needed to implicitly learn the ins and outs of our business.

Succession

Regardless of how well you think your son or daughter will do at running the family business after you are gone, you cannot simply assume that your genetic DNA is superior to anyone else's when it comes to sustaining and growing the business.

Thinking this way will be the end of you. It's a mask that you can choke yourself on without realizing it until it's too late—when suddenly you're gone and you have left this misconception that the next generation can take care of everything when they don't have the necessary entrepreneurial skills to do so. Without governance, without a constitution, how well are you prepared to overcome the interruption of a potential disaster or any type of fundamental change? Just as the human body fights microbes, or unknown organisms, with antibodies, so does the business environment fight change and the unknown.

We all have to address the change of leadership, and we need to do it sooner rather than later. We can't take ourselves out of the equation just because we feel invincible. It's a sobering process, but its one that's vital to the well-being of our families and our family business.

For the Darley family, third-generation owners of W.S. Darley & Co., choosing a successor was not an easy business.[69] Instead of

69   Business Families Foundation transcript, https://businessfamilies.org/en/
      education/p-allowing-potential-successors-to-choose-their-next-business-leader/

leaving the company to the eldest son or daughter, as many family businesses are inclined to do, CEO Bill Darley requested that his top candidates—his three sons, James, Paul, and Peter, and their cousin, Jeff—submit business plans regarding how they would continue the businesses, following Bill's death or retirement. Then he left the decision to the four of them.

"You can have rotating presidents, co-presidents, you can have one president, you can bring in a president from the outside, but I just cannot make this decision, and I am not going to rule from the grave after I am gone. So, whatever you guys come up with, I am fine with and I will support," he said, according to Paul Darley in an interview with the Business Families Foundation.

Ultimately, the team of Darleys selected Paul, based on his communication and organizational skills. "And that was very difficult for them to step back and play that second fiddle," said Paul.

But the brothers and their cousin agreed it was the best fit.

"I really think that it was a wise choice not to have me take over," said Stephen Darley. "Paul is someone who just loves the company. … His enthusiasm, his energy for the company, is what I think has really, in a lot of ways, kept us growing."

When the Family Doesn't Want the Business

As mentioned before, the transition from one generation to the next is not always successful.[70] The transfer from generation one to generation two is usually about 30 percent successful, while the percentage of successful transfers between generations two and three sits around 13 percent. The reasons can run the gamut from the next generation

---

70   "Family-Owned Business," *inc.com*, www.inc.com/encyclopedia/family-owned-businesses.html

being ill prepared to lead the company to the business just becoming no longer viable.

But what if the problem is that the next generation simply isn't interested? Or what if there *is* no next generation?

In China, this is a problem for more than half of traditional private family businesses, according to Jean Lee, codirector of the Center for Family Heritage at China Europe International Business School.

"There are theories and (real) factors that limit the willingness of the second generation to get involved. First, it is about the tide of industry," Lee told *Forbes*.[71] "Most of these family businesses are rather traditional … . Second, most went to college, and some of them went overseas and then came back … and want to set up their own company. Some of them will even choose to work for others."

Lee went on to describe a family business in which the next generation did not want to become involved, but the father faced a crisis, and his son felt he had no choice but to return. When Lee asked the son if he regretted coming back to the family business, he replied, "This is my life. It is not something that I will always enjoy but something that I am obligated to do."

So, what's the solution? In the end, you must let the members of the next generation make their own decisions. In Lee's last example, she cites the example of a son who didn't want to join the family business but instead wanted to start his own.

"We call this scenario the '1.5 Generation,'" said Lee. "So, you have not only the first generation but also the second generation, and they are cooperating with each other." By the father supporting his

---

71   Russell Flannery, "More Than Half of China's Family Businesses Face Succession Dilemma," *Forbes*, July 24, 2016, www.forbes.com/sites/russellflannery/2016/07/24/more-than-half-of-chinas-family-businesses-face-succession-dilemma/3/#7642815457b4

son in his endeavor, there's a chance that the son will eventually come back and take over the family business.

Where there's clearly no successor to a family business but the company wishes to continue on as one, or if a successor is struggling to run the business as well as it could be, then non-family managers are often brought into the fold. Family members may still sit on various governing boards, but the running of the company falls to the non-family CEO.

Take Peter Slator, CEO of century-old family business OCS. As a former divisional managing director for Rentokil Initial and a twenty-eight-year veteran of Unilever, where he served as a senior executive, Slator was welcomed to the OCS family in early 2016. The company stated that it looked forward to relying on Slator's experience and strategic abilities to drive the family-owned company into its "next chapter of development."

As for Slator, the chance to join a family business more than one hundred years old was a great opportunity. "OCS has a unique family heritage," said Slator in an OCS press release. "[As] an organization with a track record of over 115 years of growth in family ownership, I am excited about the opportunities ahead of us."[72]

In Germany, Hartmut Jenner served as CEO of the cleaning technology company Karcher, which has been family owned since its founding in 1935. Under Jenner's leadership, the company has grown financially, and its products have evolved both visually and technologically. And after fifteen years of working with the company, Jenner stated that he was starting to feel like one of the family. "Yes, the

72   "OCS Appoints New Group CEO," *OCS*, Jan 29, 2016, www.ocs.co.uk/news-article/ocs-appoints-new-group-ceo

company becomes part of the family," Jenner told *Die Presse* in 2014. "And from 11,000 [employees], I can address 4,000 by name."[73]

Finally, there are the family businesses that leave the family altogether. As we found earlier, only about one-third of family businesses make it through generational transitions, with many either selling or closing after the founder passes away.[74]

"What amazes me is the number of families that get to the designation point and the person looks up and says, 'I don't want it.' Even the most successful of businesses have these blind spots," said Stephen Salley of Banyan Family Business Advisors in an interview with the *New York Times*. "It's shocking how many families don't talk about this."[75]

According to a research study conducted by University of Warwick's Center for Competitive Advantage in the Global Economy (CAGE),[76] not only does the "death of a founding entrepreneur [wipe] out on average 60 per cent of a firm's sales and [cut] jobs by around 17 per cent," but it can also have a negative effect on the business for four years or longer after the founder's passing. This trend apparently holds across most forms of business, according to the study, from family to non-family, rural to urban.

For example, the researchers point out the impact that Steve Jobs's absence had on Apple—not just after his death in 2015, but during the decade he left the company during the 1980s and 1990s.

---

73   Rief von Norbert, "Karcher: Ich kenne 4000 Mitarbeiter beim Namen" *Die Presse*, Jan 2, 2014, http://diepresse.com/home/wirtschaft/international/1556773/ Kaercher_Ich-kenne-4000-Mitarbeiter-beim-Namen

74   "Passing on the Crown," *Economist*, Nov 4, 2004, www.economist.com/node/3352686

75   Paul Sullivan, "Tough Choices for Succession in the Family Business," *New York Times*, June 12, 2015, www.nytimes.com/2015/06/13/your-money/tough-choices-for-succession-in-the-family-business.html?_r=0

76   Sasha O. Becker and Hans K. Hvide, "Do Entrepreneurs Matter?" CAGE Working Paper No. 109/2013, www2.warwick.ac.uk/fac/soc/economics/research/centres/cage/news/07-07-14-en-trepreneurs_really_do_matter_as_study_shows_60_sales_drop_after_founders_die

"Apple struggled without him and didn't really regain its momentum until Jobs came back to the helm in the 1990s," stated Sascha O. Becker, coauthor of the study. "During this time, Jobs was lost to the firm, creating a similar dynamic to what happens in companies in which the founder-entrepreneur dies."[77]

More often than not, the problem lies in transparency. Whether the owner-founder plans to hand the company over to the next generation or sell it outside of the family, the business's structure must be organized and transparent in such a way that someone other than the founder can step in and run it.

This means creating family governance and having clear rules on how the company should be run, as well as ensuring that you have strong leadership, such as a board composed of both family and non-family members, and, finally, being rigorous on how members of the family and of the next generation can join the family business.

The fact is that not everyone in the family may be the best fit for the company, and even obvious successors of the next generation may not be ready or right for the job. This is why transparency is key, so that leadership can be taken over by whomever is most capable, not necessarily the most traditional.

As a family business owner, apart from accepting the IE that the next generation must make its own decision regarding the family business, or welcoming an external manager to run your family business, if you want your family business to stay in the family, take steps to nurture and prepare the up-and-coming generation so that they not only feel welcome but will also be aware of what "taking on the family business" will involve.

---

77   Ibid.

Preparing the Next Generation

Choosing a successor, however, is only part of the puzzle. I'm not for or against the idea, but if you're hoping to keep the business in the family, then the next generation will need to show a keen and heartfelt desire to take on that role … and that desire is not something you can force. It must be decided upon and embraced independently.

According to Stephen P. Miller, cofounder of the Family Enterprise Center at UNC Kenan-Flagler, "A positive family climate is more likely to create a safe and supportive environment for next-generation family members to take responsibility for the successes and inevitable failures that come with practicing leadership behavior."[78]

To create this environment, Miller adds, a family must focus on open communication, values and norms that are accepted by all members of the family, and a senior generation that is focused on developing the next generation, attending to their welfare, needs, and concerns, as opposed to dictating rules and wielding unquestionable authority.

In our own family business, we are constantly looking to be more transparent and open with each other and with our team members and shareholders, utilizing advances in technology for greater ease and accessibility, and we strongly support equality, both when it comes to trust and having a say in the process. As board members, my siblings and I watch out for each other, first as family members and then as family business members, but always with transparency and openness in our actions.

Additionally, it is my humble opinion that recognition is usually over-desired and under-delivered, especially in a family business. If a

---

78   Stephen P. Miller, "Developing Next-Generation Leaders in Family Business," *The Family Business Consulting Group*, www.thefbcg.com/developing-next-generation-leaders-in-family-business/

balance can be reached, it can be a key factor in the next generation's decision on whether or not to join the family business.

My father kept this balance well, recognizing in a heartfelt way those who did well, making them feel valued but never overdoing it. He did this for me numerous times, but one occasion will always stand out in my mind—the day he let me know that I was on the right track.

On that day, I was sitting in a meeting with a gentleman with whom I was negotiating a sale. As I was explaining the deal to him, I was also answering questions about our business, and at one point he asked me about our commitment to integrity.

Just then, my dad, who was in attendance, said, "He is your guy."

I was blown away. Here's my dad, a man of balanced and pointed words, publicly giving me an amazing compliment. I was so overjoyed that I felt like a little kid again, like I just rode a bike for the first time and my mom and dad were cheering for me. It's incredible how much the smallest words and gestures matter. I believe that to be even truer in family business.

I didn't act like how I was feeling, of course. I kept my cool, thanked him, and wrapped up my pitch. But after we shook hands and the prospective client left, I turned to Dad and said, "Thank you, but what did I do that was amazing? Was it my processes system? My commitment to work? My in-depth analysis?"

As always, my dad had a way to shed light on things across a wide range of angles, from the thirty-thousand-foot view to the slightest of behaviors he observed. In this case, he shook his head and said, "It was the pancakes."

"What?"

"The pancakes."

He then reminded me of an incident several years earlier when he and I were on a business trip to Europe. As we sat on the plane, I started talking to him about how I couldn't wait to get there.

"There's this one place I can't wait to visit," I said. "They have these amazing waffles and pancakes, and I'm just going to stack them up—butter, syrup, all of it. And I'm going to dig into this mountain of pancakes."

The next day we woke up and went for pancakes. It was everything I remembered—huge, fluffy pancakes dripping with butter and syrup—but as I reached out to dig in, I remembered it was my fasting day, a regimen that I have followed twice a week for the past twenty-five years to clear the mind and soul. So, I pushed it aside as quickly as I could and put the thought of it out of my mind.

"That day you showed self-restraint and self-discipline," Dad explained. "If you want me to tell you where I've seen you show these traits before, I can tell you, but the best way for me to describe it was that day with the pancakes. You were salivating. Eating those pancakes was the only thing you wanted to do. You were going in for the kill, but you suddenly realized it wasn't the right time. You knew what you wanted to do, but that action conflicted with your principles, so you put it aside. You were able to control yourself."

It was his very subtle way of telling me that resilience, discipline, and self-control are all character traits that he highly appreciated, and he projected that to me in the most amazing way through such an unassuming story that emphasized those good traits while dissuading the bad.

It reminded me that living by your principles and values makes you authentic, and others can read it in the most unassuming things. Almost all family business leaders do the same, searching for the qualities that define their ideal concept of a leader in the up-and-coming generation. That one was pointed out to me.

Clear communication combined with effective and open governance systems are invaluable in creating a fluid company structure for the next generation, giving them a clear idea of the inner workings of the business. Involvement in family meetings that focus on open communication will also give them a sense of the direction of the business and provide them with the opportunity to contribute and incite change.

"Senior generation leaders ... would be wise to provide next-generation family members with age- and experience-appropriate levels of responsibility and decision-making authority to help them gain early leadership experience, including the risk of failure that can teach valuable leadership lessons," states Miller.

Leadership opportunities for youth are diverse and start at younger ages than many realize. Take yLead, for instance. Based in a suburb of Brisbane in Queensland, Australia, the program's mission is to "support Australian schools in developing a generation of confident, motivated, and skilled young leaders who are capable and willing to make a positive difference our changing world."[79]

Starting with students as young as nine years old, yLead teaches students that "leadership is an action, not a badge" through school programs and travel that develop the students' sense of self-identity and self-confidence, their concept of the power of relationships and team dynamics, and their skills when it comes to the tools and attitudes needed to create positive change.

Take the Arcadia Preparatory School, offering the world's first Junior MBA Program for kids as young as six years old, created by its CEO Navin Valrani.

---

79   www.ylead.com.au/experiences/primary-school/

Other programs, such as the Young Presidents' Organization's Junior Leadership University, focus on developing leadership and entrepreneurial skills of YPO members' children by introducing them to other cultures.[80]

While you shouldn't try to drive your children toward joining the family business, you can greatly increase their potential contribution to the company by developing these valuable skills early. Even if they don't use them for your business, they'll be able to apply those skills toward finding a job that is personally fulfilling.

Lastly, when you say you are going to retire, plan for it! Seek a passion or hobby, or a goal with a purpose, such as philanthropy. And start early so that you have time to develop it before you step down. This will help you to really hand the leadership role over.

According to John A. Davis, founder of Cambridge Family Enterprise Group and a globally respected authority on family enterprise, wealth, leadership, and succession, "Succession is not complete until both management authority and ownership rights pass on. But they tend not to pass at the same time."[81]

It's not going to be easy to hand over the business when the time comes, all in due course, but if you have taken the time to really mentor the next generation, if you have been open with them about the entire process and included them in decision-making meetings, and if they understand the value of tapping into the senior generation's experience and advice just as Christian Weber did when he took over running Karlsberg Brauerei, then you have done what you can to engender a passion and true heart for the business in them. In the end, if they choose not to join the company, then it's for the best. Unless the succeeding generation is truly invested in driving the

---

80   www.yponyc.org/index.php?section=Member-Benefits-Education

81   "Passing on the Crown."

progress and growth of your family business into the future, then you are better off choosing a successor who is, even if they are not family.

The welfare of family, whether you're cultivating them to take over the family business one day or not, is the primary focus of the majority of family businesses. And when you're not running the day-to-day business and working to cultivate the next generation for leadership, you're likely considering how best to ensure their continued education and how to provide for the most common family needs, such as medical and maybe even funding a marriage. And until the study of life extension and genomics allows us to tack another hundred years onto our lives, we need to start planning for the next generation now, even if you're just starting your own generational cycle.[82]

In our family, as in many others, we chose to prepare for these eventual necessities instead of reacting, and we did so through studying and considering various family funds.

---

82   João Pedro de Magalhães, "The Scientific Quest for Lasting Youth: Prospects for Curing Aging," *Rejuvenation Research* 17.5 (2014): 458–467.

CHAPTER 4

Funding Family and Spirit

"In the end, we will conserve only what we love, we will love only what we understand, and we will understand only what we are taught."
—BABA DIOUM, SENEGALESE FORESTRY MINISTER

Investing in those things in life that you want to encourage in coming generations is invaluable. Funds are a means to do just this. It is a blessing to have the ability to say, "I'm going to get my education and cover my health insurance," and to know you will have the money to do those things because you or your family business has established funds for just those purposes. It's amazing, and it's something I encourage every family business to consider establishing: separate accounts that are untouched if something should happen to the business, such as if the matriarch or patriarch passes away or a business cycle comes to an end. In this chapter, I have selected to speak to some funds that other families have worked on, although there are many more to consider.

According to David Neubert of GenSpring Family Offices, "Trusts are not just for tax purposes but also for management purposes of a family business. They continue to play an important role for families" as well as provide the flexibility needed in an ever-changing operating environment.[83]

Benefits of trusts to family businesses not only include tax savings but also asset protection, asset supervision, and beneficiary protection. For instance, asset supervision can plan for a number of contingencies, from stipulating ownership on the current owner's retirement or passing, to benefits for future generations, structures for allocating educational funds, and even charitable giving.

"There's no shortage of tools business owners can use," said Bob Klosterman, CEO of White Oaks Wealth Advisors. "You have to understand the family dynamics, what you're trying to accomplish from a tax perspective, and how you want to protect beneficiaries."[84]

Funds also allow you to cultivate the next generation so that they can handle a broad range of interruptions in entrepreneurship and have the peace of mind and skills to enhance their business resources for others to benefit from. Funds are there to help out, but, as each preceding generation reminds the next, they are not to be relied upon. It is up to the members of each succeeding generation to ultimately create their own futures and to plow, plant, nurture, and harvest the fruits of their labors. In being available for these important parts of life, these funds also build the spirit, allowing for more time and resources to benefit the community and help others. In a way, these funds also fund spirits just as much, if not more, as they fund valuable parts of family lives.

---

83   Andrew Osterland, "Trusts Still Attractive to Family Business Owners," *CNBC*, Sept 22, 2014, www.cnbc.com/2014/09/18/trusts-still-attractive-to-family-business-owners.html

84   Ibid.

The idea of funds can cover an array of needs, from education, to medical, to marriage, and other key goals in between—or they can be saved for a rainy day. Whatever activities there are down the road that you think your family would benefit from engaging in, it would be wise to consider creating a fund for them.

Education Fund

An education fund can have two merits. First, it can be created to ensure that every member of the family has the money available to them to go and get an education, be it higher education or other. No family member can use "lack of funds" as an excuse not to seek learning wherever that may be, if they want to, or even for their own family constitution to guarantee a basic standard of education to those wanting to enter the business or even just to have the tools to soar alone. If you don't want or need a higher education, that's fine; the money you don't use isn't yours. It just stays in the fund. Such parameters can encourage or ease the pursuit of knowledge.

The second part of the fund can be more philanthropic. A certain amount of the fund can be set aside to help others in your community who aspire to get an education and show the ability and desire to do so but who faced hardships and challenges in high school or grade school, or at any point, that made earning the next step in education more difficult.

It is a fund that is giving to the society around you and helps your family at the same time. In addition, the fund can be used for "educational experiences," such as funding internships for promising candidates who may not have the formal education but have the skills and abilities and desire to do well at one of your companies.

Pierre Choueiri, CEO of the family-run Choueiri Group, a leading media representation group in the Middle East and North Africa, had a similar idea when he founded the Pierre Choueiri Family Fund for Global Family Enterprise at the D'Amore–McKim School of Business.

"When my father passed the company to me, it was the proudest day of my life," said Choueiri. "But in today's business climate, education is essential to understanding complex issues faced by family-owned businesses—management succession, ownership control, shareholder relationships—so that the family is running the company, not just owning it."[85]

To that end, Choueiri wanted to ensure that students at D'Amore-McKim, including those from family businesses all over the world as well as his own two children, would have a chance to develop these specialized skills. His oldest son, Antoine, attended the school as a business major at the time of the fund's establishment, and his son Alex planned to major in the music industry when he began at the school.

"The Choueiri gift ... will generate research that provides the insights necessary to shape successful family enterprises for generations," said Hugh Courtney, dean of D'Amore-McKim.

Another example is the Flora Family Foundation, founded by Hewlett-Packard Company cofounder William R. Hewlett and his wife, Flora, in 1998. The foundation is also a strong supporter of education, granting funds to numerous endowments, program initiatives, and fellowships all over the world.[86]

---

85 Empower Campaign, "Parents Give a Boost to Family Business Education," *Northeastern University*, www.northeastern.edu/empower/news/ parents-give-a-boost-to-family-business-education

86 www.florafamily.org/about.html

The foundation is particularly close to the Hewlett family, with decisions on the organization of the foundation as well as where funds should be allocated being made by both a Family Council, consisting of the founders' children and grandchildren and their spouses, as well as a board of directors composed of family members and two non-family members.

In regard to funding education, the foundation "puts the K–12 age group at the forefront of its education investments," according to *Inside Philanthropy*, and at its core, the foundation believes that "each individual has an obligation to go beyond the narrow confines of his or her personal interests and be mindful of the broader concerns of humanity."[87]

Research and Development/ Intellectual Development Fund

Apart from a family education fund, creating a fund to sponsor the intellectual development of promising team members can be invaluable. Proactive education for training team members or helping to improve their knowledge in specific fields not only benefits them but also positions them as an even more valuable asset in your company.

Take BMW, a family business owned by the Quandt family and one of the top ten largest family businesses in the world, as of 2014.[88] To develop the talent and skills of its employees, the German car manufacturer began building alliances with universities, working

---

87   "Flora Family Foundation: Grants for K-12 Education," www.insidephilanthropy.com/grants-for-
      k-12-education/flora-family-foundation-grants-for-k-12-education.html

88   James Lee, "Top 10 Largest Family Businesses in the World," *Tharawat Magazine*, June 1,
      2015, www.tharawat-magazine.com/facts/top-10-largest-family-businesses-world/#gs.jsAL2SY

with the schools to create talent development programs and even a doctoral degree in automotive engineering.[89, 90]

At Clemson University in South Carolina, for instance (which is located less than fifty miles from BMW's only plant in North America), the automaker was able to work with the school to develop the curriculum for an automotive engineering graduate degree, allowing students and professors to work alongside BMW engineers to learn the intricacies of designing, developing, building, and even marketing the kind of high-tech, high-end vehicles that BMW is known for today.[91]

The intellectual development of team members, and the funding of research and development to not only improve team member knowledge base but also to benefit the development of the family company's intellectual property, is "widely regarded [by family-controlled corporations] as an essential factor for achieving and sustaining a competitive advantage through innovation," according to research conducted by Ivan Miroshnychenko of the Sant'Anna School of Advanced Studies in Pisa, Italy.[92] In fact, "Family-owned firms have demonstrated an ability to innovate in almost every industry, from agriculture to space engineering," and additional research has suggested that "family firms are able to develop a unique composition of organizational resources together with knowledge structures and knowledge combinability that enhances their R&D investment behavior."

89 "Strategic University Co-Operations," *BMW*, www.bmwgroup.com/en/company/university-cooperations.html

90 Lynnley Browning, "BMW's Custom Made University," *New York Times*, Aug 29, 2006, www.nytimes.com/2006/08/29/business/worldbusiness/29bmw.html

91 Ibid.

92 Ivan Miroshnychenko, "Founders' Voices R&D Investment Behavior in Family-Controlled Corporations in Europe," *WZB*, March 2014, www.wzb.eu/sites/default/files/publikationen/wzb_mitteilungen/s36-38miroshynko.pdf

Looking to the next generation of family business owners, innovation and research and development are two of the key areas that the up-and-coming generation plans to invest in, with 76 percent of respondents listing "innovation" as a "top three priority," according to the Deloitte EMEA Family Business Centre.[93]

The study adds that family businesses may be able to innovate at faster rates than non-family companies "because they are not driven by the short-term interests of external investors and capital markets, and can spend more money on research and development."

According to the US Department of Labor, the workplaces that result in higher performance levels offer their employees "incentives, information, skills, and responsibility to make decisions essential for innovation, quality improvement, and rapid response to change."[94]

In Washington, DC, family-owned construction company Shapiro & Duncan "invest[s] substantially in apprenticeship programs and … a wide variety of other career development and educational opportunities," according to an article in *Constructor Magazine* by S&D team members Geoff Phillips and Sarah Mueller.[95]

The educational development of its employees is such a priority for S&D that it even dubbed its training and development sector the S&D YOUniverity.

For S&D, the drive to include more education was based on the decreasing workforce, with half a million unfilled positions as of 2016, and workers aged forty to upper-fifties choosing to leave the

93   Deloitte EMEA Family Business Centre, "Next-Generation Family Businesses: Evolution Keeping Family Values Alive" *Deloitte*, May 2016, www2.deloitte.com/content/dam/Deloitte/global/Documents/Strategy/gx-family-business-nextgen-survey.pdf

94   www.oeockent.org/resources-events/selling-to-your-employees/whats-an-esop/creating-ownership-culture/

95   Geoff Phillips and Sarah Mueller, "S&D YOUniversity Is Foundation for Mechanical Contractor's Commitment to Employee Education, Training and Development," *Constructor*, http://www.constructormagazine.com/sd-youniversity-is-foundation-for-mechanical-contractors-commitment-to-employee-education-training-and-development/#.WDRYX6IrJTY

industry in increasing numbers. "As a result, the construction jobs deficit is expected to increase to 2 million by 2022."[96]

A large part of this deficit, the article states, is due to the perception that there is little option for advancement in the construction industry, a myth that S&D hopes to put to rest with its educational programs. At S&D YOUniversity, "a plumber can become a project manager, or an HVAC technician can become an estimator. An apprentice can become a foreman, then an assistant project manager, then a project manager. From there, the career path could lead to project executive and ultimately to vice president. It all depends on the individual's attitude, ambition, and aptitude."

Along with YOUniversity training, S&D also offers a tuition reimbursement at nearby Montgomery College or the University of Maryland for up to two credits annually, and includes training offerings at its main office, in the field (for training in areas such as excavation and heavy equipment operation), and online.

Ultimately, the family-owned company considers its YOUniversity to be a win-win across the board. "Any business is comprised of the people in that business, and the success of the company is ultimately driven by those people. That's why it is so critically important to invest in employees, just as a business invests in IT infrastructure, new equipment or facility improvements. Employee education, training, and development should be viewed as a strategic investment opportunity."[97]

Marriage Fund

They say that marriage is one of the biggest investments (financial and certainly otherwise!) you can make as an adult, along with

---

96   Ibid.

97   Ibid.

having kids and buying a house. Not everyone wants to get married, but if one wishes to get married, what a great option it is to have a marriage fund!

As opposed to the education fund, the marriage fund is a set amount adjusted for inflation that a family member can use for their wedding.

Interestingly enough, the United Arab Emirates, which comprises seven emirates each governed by a family monarch, has a marriage fund for UAE nationals.[98] Created in 1992 following the social policy developed by the late Sheikh Zayed bin Sultan Al Nahyan, the mission of the fund is to "provide future spouses with the financial support as well as preparing and qualifying them with the skills and knowledge required for the establishment of a coherent and stable Emirati family." Ultimately, the vision of the fund is to "build and support coherent and stable families in the UAE." That's what I call a social program with a noble goal!

Marriage funds can be any size, from a small set amount to a variable calculated for inflation, if the fund is in place over multiple generations. Either way, having this fund available can help ease the minds of senior generations as their children's potential weddings—and the inevitable high costs associated with them—approach.

Medical Fund

When it comes to medical costs, even with the best medical insurance you can get, no one can tell if their system or alternative ones are the best fit, but an emergency fund can go a long way to alleviate

---

98   www.abudhabi.ae/portal/public/en/departments/department_detail?docName=
       ADEGP _DF_14362_EN&_adf.ctrl-state=q3z9p7h6w_4&_afrLoop=
       9519599792409967#!

those worries, especially when there are still going to be deductibles to cover and other unexpected out-of-pocket expenses.

In the case of a family member passing, the fund can also help the surviving spouse manage life expenses until the lengthy and often costly legal processes are complete.

Additionally, the fund can pay for the cost of deliveries. Insurance, of course, pays for most of that, but the fund could go above and beyond to help with more difficult or complicated births, or to pay for a qualified nanny to help out over time.

In the United States, family-controlled Ford Motor Company is one of many large-scale companies that use a standalone tax-exempt Welfare Benefit Trust called a Voluntary Employees' Beneficiaries Association, or VEBA, to pre-fund employee benefits, such as health insurance, in a way that allows the trust to assume employer's liability for benefits under the plan.[99]

In the United States, the option of a Welfare Benefit Trust (WBT) can be used by family businesses to increase their team members' benefits. Benefits paid by the trust can include insurance, such as medical, disability and life, dental and vision coverage, severance pay, and others, and can be an additional benefit to existing medical coverage. For the family business, the benefit of using a WBT is in tax benefits and deductions,

"If you create a WBT, it can allow the family business to pre-fund the cost of certain employer benefits," states Charles Epstein, an investment advisor and founder of Epstein Financial Group. "A VEBA welfare benefit trust can receive tax-free earnings on the amounts put into the trust, which can reduce benefit costs." Epstein

---

99   Andrew Stumpff, "The 'Big Three' VEBAs and Other Stand-Alone Welfare Benefit Trusts: What Is Novel and Not," *Bloomberg BNA*, Dec. 8, 2009, www.bna.com/big-three-vebas-n2147484315/

adds that, "A WBT can also, in some cases, allow you to take a tax deduction when you could not previously do so without the trust."[100]

There are plenty of other benefits and limitations to these types of trusts, and certainly other types of trusts out there, but the point is that there are options for funding your team members' medical needs outside of traditional health insurance coverage in ways that protect and even benefit your family business while investing in your biggest asset: your team members.

Investment Fund

I have spoken of our investment fund in previous chapters, and essentially this fund is the one we use to encourage entrepreneurship and diversification of business. It was a great idea that my parents introduced, and it has unified my siblings and me because it requires that we work together.

That is, based on a formula and when feasible, there is a portion of money that we can use to invest in potentially good prospects. No one person can make this decision on his or her own. We as a family entity have to collectively agree that this prospect works for us as a whole. We quickly learned to compromise. We learned to listen to the other side, and whichever business we decide to invest in, we do, ultimately, in the interest of continuity.

I was able to make good use of our family's investment fund early on to launch a trading company that I originally set out to create entirely on my own. It was early on in my career, and back then I thought I needed to flap my own wings before flying with the flock. At the time, I was confident that the banker who served

---

100   Charles Epstein, "How a Welfare Benefit Trust Can Reduce Your Company's Costs," *Family Business Center of Pioneer Valley*, http://fambizpv.com/articles/money_issues/welfare_benefit_ trust.html last accessed July 11, 2017

my father would be just as excited to work with me. But once I was on my own without my father's and family's support, it was a different story.

I went into that one-on-one meeting with the banker to secure facilities for my own independent proposal. However, what I got out of that meeting was a lesson: It is not just about name association but rather the values of reputation, networking, branding, and the importance of being a part of something bigger.

"Being your father's son and being associated with his group is one thing," the banker explained to me, "but to fund you on your own is not the same. I can give you advice about the idea, but that's it."

You cannot form a strong reputation, connections, and a solid network overnight. It takes time to build. Fortunately, I was able to turn to the family investment fund and get my siblings on board with the idea of the company, and we were able to do it together, which is another great benefit of this fund: learning and growing in your ability to work with others … and especially with family. Of course, I'm not saying that one can't do this on his or her own; they certainly can. But through my experience, I was able to learn about and appreciate the power of the collective.

If my siblings or I have a viable idea, we do it together, and the one who originated the idea gets remuneration for proposing it. It's a form of royalty that allows all of us to benefit from our collective perspectives and ideas, and also permits us to take on interruptions, to contemplate different views and different concepts that we study, consider, and review. If we end up putting the concept in place, then we all benefit in a way that creates unity.

Because of the investment fund, we found ourselves going to China, looking at opportunities in the African continent and Asia, and getting into different types of businesses. The important part was that everyone felt that they had a voice that would be heard—that we could do it together, collectively.

In the Netherlands, the Van Eeghen Group is a prime example of a company that has remained open to new investment opportunity proposals from the family, adapting to new circumstances and providing for customers' needs as the market fluctuated over the years.[101]

From their early years in the trading industry, to starting a bank in North America in the late 1700s, to dealing in dehydrated foods in the 1960s, and "functional foods" such as vitamins and probiotics in the early 1990s, when it comes to considering new business directions, the 350-year-old family-owned company is surprisingly agile. Until recent years, the company has relied on a board of family members to keep their ears to the ground on innovative new business concepts and approaches, with results that have proven advantageous time and again.

Another family company, Rudin Management in New York City, was known for years for its cautious investments and long-term view, which has been referenced to time and again in an oft-quoted anecdote.

The story goes that founder Lew Rudin was playing a game of Monopoly at a charity breakfast, and even though he appeared to be losing, he ended up having far more cash at the end of the game than any of the other players.[102] According to later reports, Rudin's strategy was to "invest conservatively and save his money so that he could scoop up more valuable real estate later."[103]

---

101 www.henokiens.com/userfiles/file/Cas_Van_Eeghen.pdf

102 Konrad Putzier, "For Family Dynasties: Adapt or Die: Real estate families are shaking up strategies and battling forces, like REITs and private equity, to stay relevant," *The Real Deal*, Aug 1, 2015, http://therealdeal.com/issues_articles/for-family-dynasties-adapt-or-die/

103 Ibid.

This approach to real estate investing lasted until well after Lew Rudin's passing in 2001, but by the mid-2010s, his sons Bill and Jack, and grandson Eric, had revitalized the company by investing in several forward-thinking ventures, including the development of a 675,000-square-foot office building in the Brooklyn Navy Yard for WeWork Cos., a collaborative workspace that Bill Rudin referred to as "the future of real estate," and a real estate technology venture called Digital Building Operating System, or Di-BOSS.[104, 105]

The heating and air conditioning management in particular had already increased energy efficiency in two of Rudin's buildings by 30 percent during the pilot phase and resulted in savings of $505,000 for Rudin just during the winter of 2012–13.

For the Rudin family, investing in the development of the Di-BOSS system was a risk, but it was one that the family business was happy it made.

"We are always trying to improve on what we're doing," said Michael Rudin, the Rudin family member who is getting Di-BOSS up and running as a separate company. "Getting comfortable is very easy to do, but fortunately we've steered clear of that."[106]

Philanthropy Fund

When you've been blessed with any kind of success, in business or otherwise, one of the greatest things you can do is pay it forward.

In many cultures, it is encouraged to take a percentage of the earnings you have made and contribute that to charity. It is a mor-

104   Roger Anderson, "Di-BOSS: the World's First Digital Building Operating System" *Earth Institute*, Aug 16, 2013, http://blogs.ei.columbia.edu/2013/08/16/38968/

105   "WeWork Brooklyn Project Gets Backing from Big Developers," *Bloomberg*, July 2015, www.bloomberg.com/news/articles/2015-07-06/wework-brooklyn-project-gets-backing-from-big-developers

106   Putzier, "For Family Dynasties."

alistic obligation, not a requirement, and it is one that my parents chose to participate in as they could. In doing so, they taught us that giving is ultimately more rewarding than receiving, and that feeling of reward lasts even beyond death. This is not unique to one culture but to many across the globe.

In South Los Angeles, California, the passing of E. J. Jackson, owner of the family business Jackson Limousine, sent a shockwave through the community and prompted heartfelt comments from community activists to the city mayor and even House Representative Maxine Waters.

"E. J. Jackson was one of the kindest, most generous human beings that I've ever met in my life. [He] worked very hard to be of assistance to families, to children, and … he was doing this all year," said Waters.[107]

Jackson, who came from a homeless background, began his limousine business in South Los Angeles when he noticed that many luxury car services were denying service to his predominantly black community. And as his service grew, so did his charitable giving.

In 1982, Jackson hosted his first turkey dinner giveaway, just a few days before Thanksgiving—an event that soon became one of Southern California's most prominent holiday charity events.[108] Over the years, thousands of families have received Thanksgiving groceries through the giveaway, which started with a few hundred turkeys given away and grew to 12,000 meals donated as of 2016.

"The holidays in L.A. won't be the same without E. J. on the streets at sunrise, making sure everyone's basket is full," said Los

---

107   Makeda Easter, "E. J. Jackson, South L.A. businessman Known for Annual Thanksgiving Turkey Giveaways, Dies at 66," *Los Angeles Times*, Nov 3, 2016, www.latimes.com/local/lanow/la-me-ln-ej-jackson-death-20161103-story.html

108   Jonathan Lloyd and Kim Baldonado, "LA Limo Service Founder, Organizer of Thanksgiving Turkey Giveaway Dies" *NBC News Channel 4*, Nov 2, 2016, www.nbclosangeles.com/news/local/EJ-Jackson-Turkey-Giveaway-Charity-Holiday-Limousine-Service-399644611.html

Angeles Mayor Eric Garcetti. "He set a timeless example for us to follow, and we can honor his legacy by building on the tradition he started and committing ourselves every day to making a difference in the lives of our families, friends, and neighbors."[109]

Although Jackson was most known for his Thanksgiving charity, he was also a regular visitor to L.A.'s homeless camps, taking food and water, and he hired people from his community that had trouble finding work.

"He was an aspirational person who believed in giving community members a second chance," said community activist Najee Ali.

"His legacy will live on," said E. J.'s youngest son, Tyron. "I learned so much from him."[110]

My father was also a deeply giving man, though he never spoke about it. Following is an example of unspoken giving.

During my father's funeral, a man who had known him well came up to me. He was a man of the cloth. He asked me if I'd noticed that he was not in attendance on the third day of the condolences and proceeded to say:

"I had to attend a conference. After I finished the second day of the condolence, I left at eight p.m. and went by my office to get some papers before leaving the next day. As I arrived at my office, I saw a man sitting on a bench in front of my office, crying.

"'What's wrong, brother?' I asked him. "'How can I help you?'

"The man was holding a newspaper in his hand and was in such a state that he couldn't speak clearly. He simply pointed to the picture in the paper.

"It was a picture of your father, along with the announcement of his passing. The man was crying and clutching your father's picture

---

109 Ibid.

110 Easter, "E.J. Jackson."

in his hands. When he finally calmed down enough to speak, he said between sobs, 'This man used to help me every time I went to the factory. He would come and give me a hand, and he was always there for me during difficult times. I didn't know he was the owner of the business. I didn't know what his name was. All I knew was what he did for me, and now he's gone.'"

I walked away with tears in my eyes and thought about the odds of that man being in front of that office at just that time, learning about my father's passing at just that moment, and this holy man taking the time to come and tell me the story was like a gentle but powerful voice from beyond the grave: "Remember, son, you have to do good."

That is the kind of impact one wants to have when they engage in charity. It is not the bragging right, not for people to know about. It's the feeling that you know that you are changing people's lives for the better. Even beyond the grave, you have an impact. No matter where you are in life, you can do something good.

According to Strategic Philanthropy president Betsy Brill, "Businesses that are owned or controlled by families are using philanthropy as part of a business strategy and aligning the family's core values with the company's. It make sense and can also be extremely beneficial to business objectives such as attracting and retaining great employees and improving the company's reputation as a good corporate citizen with its customers, community, vendors, and suppliers."[111]

---

111   Charls Paikert, "Stepping Up at Family Firms," *New York Times*, Nov 8, 2012, www.nytimes. com/2012/11/09/giving/more-family-firms-make-philanthropy-their-business.html

CHAPTER 5

The Power of Giving and the Strength of Community

"The best way to find yourself is to lose yourself in the service of others."
—MAHATMA GANDHI

This chapter is meant to expand on the concept of philanthropy as a fund, because it is so significant. The idea of it, and how it resonates in my life, can be summed up in one incident that happened during a family trip in the States.

This may sound spoiled, but for the longest time, I was not a fan of leftover food. I did not like to get doggie bags at restaurants because I refused to eat leftovers. And yet, after enjoying a lovely dinner with my family at a seaside restaurant in L.A. some years ago, I found myself holding a doggie bag while my wife played with our young daughters on the nearby boardwalk.

I was an arm's swing away from tossing the doggie bag in the bin when I saw a man roll by me in a wheelchair, park, and bring out his dinner.

His dinner was what stopped me. As I watched, he pulled out one thin round piece of bread and carefully cut a triangle about the size of two fingers from it, saving the rest for later. Then he opened a small box of fast food barbeque sauce and dipped his bread in it, savoring every little bite.

I felt horrendous. Here I had this big box of food, still hot from the restaurant, and I was going to toss it in the trash because I had this ridiculous preconception in my head about leftovers.

I pointed out the man to my wife, and she walked up and greeted him. I saw her hold up the bag, telling him that our family just enjoyed a wonderful dinner but that we ordered too much. The kids weren't hungry and the food was fresh—would he please accept it?

Even though the man was obviously hungry, he still looked her up and down and seriously considered whether or not he'd take the food. In the end, because he could see me and the girls waiting for her not too far away, he accepted it, said thank you, and gently hung it on the side of his wheelchair before rolling away.

My girls fell into my arms, crying, because of the scene unfolding in front of their eyes. Their compassion was heartwarming, and suddenly they wanted to give everyone something. There was a joy in them that hadn't been there a moment ago, a sense of reward in helping someone who truly needed it.

When you're doing something for one person or for society, or doing something for your neighborhood or for a particular cause that is close to you, taking a moment to address an interruption that few things can ever really compare to. You can receive all the riches in the world, and it will never compare to the joy you receive when you give back. Would it not be divine for one to have his own Mass Transformative Purpose, such as giving back to the community? But we can better give if we have a profitable business. As such, giving can be an incredibly positive IE—a change in business that is an opportunity to turn your success into joy.

There are many means of helping others. My maternal grandfather took joy in giving clothing or books to students of his who were in need. More often than not, the student never found out who gave them those much-needed supplies. Giving doesn't have to be extravagant. There are avenues to be charitable with simple things, such as a kind word or a tap of support on the shoulder. Education alone is a great value.

However you chose to give, just the act of it can make the biggest difference. Take the "zoom in, zoom out" perspective, where one looks at the immensity of the universe and then compares that to the immensity of atomic emptiness, zooming from the outer reaches of the galactic spiral to the relative size of quarks within a nucleus. It would seem that any action in such vast spaces would be inconsequential, but that is the furthest thing from the truth. Nothing more than the excitation of electrons can create laser beams capable of conducting eye surgery, and the action of stars dozens of light-years from Earth can have dramatic effects on our planet. But so, too, in a positive way, can the smallest action of kindness have the grandest impact on our world.

Giving for Protection

I speak about Marilyn Carlson Nelson in the chapter on Gender Empowerment (Chapter 7), but I would be remiss not to bring her up here for her amazing contributions in philanthropy and particularly in her drive to end human trafficking. As former chairman and chief executive officer of the worldwide travel and hospitality family company Carlson, Nelson represented her company as the first signatory on an International Code of Conduct that pledged that her company would do its part to educate its employees on the issue of human trafficking and would take reasonable action to prevent the illicit activity.

"I was counseled by several colleagues and PR experts that this was too unsavory an issue with which to be associated and that it might implicate us in a negative way in the consumers' mind," said Nelson in her book *How We Lead Matters*. "I listened, and then I traveled to the United Nations, and I signed the code."[112]

Nelson is also the cofounder of the World Childhood Foundation,[113] which serves to protect street children around the world from human trafficking, and has served on the boards of the United National Global Compact, the Committee Encouraging Corporate Philanthropy, and the National Endowment for Democracy.

Giving for the Greater Family

In Dubai, the al-Ghurair family, which invests in a number of different companies around the world, created an IE in their family business when they made a significant contribution to the Arab world in 2016 with the launch of an education fund amounting to $1.14 billion in grants to help Middle Eastern students who qualify for top universities but are unable to afford them.[114] The fund, which comprises nearly one-third of the al-Ghurair family wealth, is built

---

112 Marilyn Carlson Nelson, *How We Lead Matters: Reflections on a Life of Leadership* (New York: McGraw-Hill, 2008), 101.

113 www.carlson.com/cdc-cms/pdf/Bios/Marilyn percent20Carlson percent20Nelson percent20Bio. pdf

114 Aya Batrawy, "UAE Tycoon Launches Largest Arab Education Fund with $1.14B," *AP*, April 20, 2016. http://bigstory.ap.org/article/093a43bb609c4e808c70cf6b38d261a4/ uae-tycoon-launches-largest-arab-education-fund-114b

as a perpetual endowment, and while it is expected to help at least 15,000 students over ten years, it is intended to last well beyond that.

"It [the educational fund] had to be significant in size. It has to make an impact on the region," said fund chairman Abdul Aziz al-Ghurair.[115]

As of 2014, the Middle East had the world's highest youth unemployment rates, due partially to the lack of access to jobs and quality education.

The al-Ghurair family's reason for creating the fund, Abdul Aziz stated, was because the prosperity of the Arab world can only come through proper education. "Our legacy is we made our wealth from this region, from the UAE, and we want to contribute to the society."[116]

Giving to the Community

In Australia, the Cuteri family of Turi Foods rose from humble Italian immigrant roots to build a family of businesses that provide quality cheeses and poultry throughout the country, and in 2010 they opened their philanthropic division: the Turi Trust.

The Turi Trust is designed to encourage Turi employees to become more involved in their communities, helping those organizations that "care for those in need in Australia and abroad with a particular emphasis on children and young adults."[117] The program assists in this support by offering employees the opportunity to give back either by direct donation, product donation, or other means.

Over the years, the fund has supported multiple charities, including Leukodystrophy Australia and Northern Hospital in

---

115   Ibid.

116   Ibid.

117   http://turifoods.com.au/community/turi-trust.html

Victoria, which has praised the Trust for their regular donations and sponsorships.

"We believe in having strong ties with our community," said Pina Di Donato, director of the Turi Trust and daughter of Turi founder, Sam Cuteri, in an interview with Northern Hospital. "At Turi Foods, we work and live in this community, and we believe we have a responsibility to give back."[118]

"We believe it's really important for local businesses and the community to support our health services as best we can," Pina added. "It's up to us to work together as a community."[119]

The Giving Nature of Family Businesses

It may not be surprising to find out that family businesses are more likely to give back to their communities, with more than 50 percent reporting "a high commitment to corporate social responsibility [CSR] and sustainability practices," and more than 80 percent engaged in philanthropy on at least some level, according to a joint study conducted by Ernst & Young Global Limited (EY) and Kennesaw State University.[120] The study goes on to note that family businesses are much more likely—85 percent—to have a code of ethics, compared to only 57 percent of the world's largest companies.

The report also points out that supporting CSR in a family business is a strong driver of family pride and better company performance overall.

---

118   www.nhfoundation.org.au/2011/10/the-turi-trust-supporting-
      future-generations/

119   My appreciation also goes to the late YPO international chapter chair Santiago Sanchez, whose
      enthusiasm to serve and give inspired a generation of YPOers.

120   "Staying Power: How Do Family Businesses Create Lasting Success?" *Ernst & Young Global
      Limited and Kennesaw State University study.* 2015. www.ey.com/Publication/vwLUAssets/ey-
      staying-power-how-do-family-businesses-create-lasting-success/$FILE/ey-staying-power-how-
      do-family-businesses-create-lasting-success.pdf

"They're not just a public relations exercise," the report stated. "They [sustainability and CSR practices] tend to result in increased operational efficiency, reduced waste, and increased product differentiation, which helps to improve business processes and profitability."[121]

Take the work of the Fuente family, for example. Known worldwide for their fine cigars, Carlos "Carlito" Fuente Jr. of the Fuente Companies, founders of Arturo Fuente Cigars, received the 2014 Humanitarian Award from Variety - the Children's Charity for his efforts in creating the Cigar Family Charitable Foundation. I had the pleasure to meet and bond with Carlito during a visit to the Dominican Republic, thanks to my dear friend, Mohammed Mohebi. It was an amazing experience - while the foundation was first established to provide clean water and an elementary school to the region surrounding the family farm, it has since grown to include a medical and dental clinic, community health and clean water programs, vocational training support, sports facilities, a community kitchen, and even the means of maintaining local infrastructure, such as roads and bridges. The Foundation actively helps more than 450 students, along with its support of the rest of the nearby community, and has been recognized as a model charity in the Caribbean by the United Nations.

Giving back to the community is also very conducive to the long-term goals of a family business. There is an inherent symbiotic relationship at work in supporting their community. The community, in return, is more likely to support the family business, which encourages more support on behalf of the family business, and so on. It is a perpetual cycle of good that only grows stronger over time as communities not only drive more support for the business but also as the

---

121 Ibid.

family and team members of the company feel increasing pride in their charitable deeds.

Giving back to society is one of the greatest things that any family business can do. It is a solution to a situation or community interruption using entrepreneurial spirit that not only gives you a deep sense of fulfillment, but it also results in good blessings from the community around you. It improves your surrounding environment, if even just a little bit, and makes things just that much better. It is paying forward at its most basic level—if you do a little bit, it encourages the next person to do the same, and so on.

The 700 Return and Creating 'Zero Gap'

Many people believe that what you do comes back to you in multitudes. For instance, some subscribe to the idea that if you give a dollar to charity, God will bestow blessing on you up to seven hundred times that amount. How and when and where, you don't know, but it encourages you to do that good because you believe it will return. And in the desire to do good, we all have a common wish. How many things can we list where we all share a common desire?

For the Rockefeller Foundation, creating return while also having a strong impact on society and the environment is the basic theory behind their "Impact Investing" concept. Essentially, the Impact Investment concept works by creating financing mechanisms that draw from large pools of private capital to support innovations that "have the potential to create outsized impact."

For instance, financiers have used impact investing to create:

- More efficiently designed models for vaccine funding

- More consistent funding streams for treating malaria, tuberculosis, and HIV/AIDS

- An uptick in the financing of green investments

- Greater availability of affordable childhood vaccines[122,123]

According to Lorenzo Bernasconi, senior associate director of the Rockefeller Foundation, "Large and entrenched social, economic, and environmental challenges are invariably accompanied by large and entrenched market failures. Finding financial solutions that overcome these market failures requires an ability to commit resources, take on risk, and assume a long-term horizon. Philanthropy is uniquely positioned to do this."[124]

For its part, the Rockefeller Foundation is putting significant resources toward its "Zero Gap" program, an impact investment finance portfolio that uses a venture philanthropy model to encourage the elements of innovation—creativity, risk-taking, patience, collaboration, resources, and grit—in an effort to achieve systemic change in sustainable global development.

Two organizations that the Zero Gap program has invested in as of 2015 are the World Bank City Creditworthiness Initiative, which focuses on helping cities fund climate-smart infrastructure and services, and the Extreme Climate Facility, which is working to build climate resilience and adaptation in Africa, a country known for its weather-related disasters.

Additional funding mechanisms that the Zero Gap initiative is exploring include methods of raising capital from commercial institutions for environmental preservation, as well as micro-levies designed to fund the fight against childhood malnutrition.

---

122   www.rockefellerfoundation.org/blog/development-goals-without-money-are-just-a-dream/

123   www.rockefellerfoundation.org/our-work/initiatives/innovative-finance/

124   www.rockefellerfoundation.org/insights/
       insights-detail/#why-should-philanthropy-be-involved-with-innovative-finance

"New partnership and business models are often at the core of new solutions for channeling private sector capital for social good," stated Adam Connaker, program associate for the Rockefeller Foundation. "Philanthropy has a unique role to play in bringing together the required actors from across business, government, and the nonprofit sector to forge these new solutions."[125]

Another group that's focusing on societal benefits, job creation, positive interruptions, and environmental preservation is ZERI (Zero Emissions Research and Initiatives), a global network that works mainly with large and small family companies for the purpose of "seek[ing] sustainable solutions for society, from unreached communities to corporations inspired by nature's design principles."[126]

To achieve this, ZERI has developed a philosophy called Blue Economy, which uses innovative business models to bring "competitive products and services to the market [that respond] to basic needs while building social capital" and also helping the environment.

There are hundreds of innovative ideas documented on Blue Economy's website (www.theblueeconomy.org), each of which presents information on a potential market, innovation, and opportunity. For instance, one study documents the potential to use certain silks with a higher tensile strength than titanium as a biodegradable replacement for razors, which currently comprise about 100,000 tons of landfill. Not only would this innovation reduce landfill, but it would also allow for the planting of an estimated 1,250,000 trees to raise silk-producing bugs and create around 1.5 million jobs in the silk processing industry.

125 www.rockefellerfoundation.org/insights/
     insights-detail/#why-should-philanthropy-be-involved-with-innovative-finance

126 Risk Reduction Foundation, "Gunter Pauli: 'The world needs a new economic system—the best has to be the cheapest,'" *Risk Reduction Foundation*, 2012, http://rr-f.ch/en/media/37

Another study looks at the societal and economic benefits of reusing coffee waste for the production of edible tropical mushrooms, the demand for which is quickly increasing across the globe. About 99.7 percent of coffee biomass is discarded in the harvesting process, which is a massive waste when you consider that the world consumed about 7.5 million tons of coffee in 2009 alone.

Instead of wasting coffee castaways, one solution is to use this biomass to grow valuable mushrooms such as shiitake and ganoderma, which thrive and even sprout earlier on logs created from coffee by-production, including the pruning, husks, pulp, and grounds. Once the mushrooms are harvested, the leftovers, which are now rich with the enzyme lysine, can be used for quality animal feed.

This process has already been adopted by Equator Coffees & Teas, which offers its coffee waste to BTTR Ventures, which in turn farms mushrooms on the waste and also offers urban mushroom farming kits for purchase.

In fact, Equator has taken the coffee/mushroom relationship even further by creating a blend to support the efforts of Chido Govero, who teaches women in Zimbabwe how to use the coffee waste from local farms to grow mushrooms.

According to Blue Economy's report, "First the women, most of them single mothers, orphans, and elderly, gain access to protein based on local and readily available resources. This creates jobs, and the combination of work and food is often all what is needed to stop the abuse of women. If women are respected at all ages, then it puts the brakes on sex trade, and even reduces the risks of AIDS at the core of society."[127]

---

127   Pauli Gunter, Pauli, "Beyond CSR (Corporate Social Responsibility)," *Blue Economy report*, 2010, www.theblueeconomy.org/uploads/7/1/4/9/71490689/case_32_beyond_corporate_social_respo.pdf

Blue Economy continues to generate business models such as this one, aimed at benefiting both society and the environment while also offering the potential for significant revenue, in the hopes that the "material will continue to engender exchanges and the desire to take action ... [inspiring] the young at heart and in age to become entrepreneurs who want to make a difference."

Charity Incognito

In the end, philanthropy is about giving back and doing something good without the need for recognition. However, in this section I will call out a few names.

Margaret Cargill, of the well-known agricultural family business Cargill, surprised the world when she left $6 billion to a number of charities on her passing in 2006, including the American Red Cross, YMCA, and the Public Broadcasting Service, as well as numerous elder care, child care, and animal care organizations, and environmental nonprofits.

According to an article in *The Chronicle of Philanthropy*, Margaret did not like being recognized for her charitable work and even stated in her will that her trustees shouldn't "even think of cranking up the PR machine" when her donations were distributed.[128]

The Murugappa family of the Murugappa Group, a conglomerate that focuses on a number of commodities from sugars and fertilizers to bicycles and financial services has a long history of philanthropy.[129] Starting with the creation of a hospital in his native village of Pallathur, India, in 1924, Murugappa Group founder Dewan

---

128   Maria Di Mento, "Donors Who Gave the Most in 2011 – No 1; Margaret Cargill," *The Chronicle of Philanthropy*, Feb 6, 2012, www.philanthropy.com/article/No-1-Margaret-A-Cargill/157273

129   https://en.wikipedia.org/wiki/Murugappa_family

A.M.M. Murugappa Chettiar "strongly believed that personal well-being was meaningless without social welfare."[130]

In 1953, the Murugappa family started the A.M.M. Foundation, a philanthropic organization dedicated to improving health care and education in rural and underdeveloped communities in India. As of 2013, the foundation currently ran four hospitals located in areas near where the Murugappa Group operated, seeing close to 15,000 inpatients and 750,000 outpatients annually. It also ran four schools and one polytechnic college, working with the government to fund two of the schools to provide education to children from less-privileged homes and subsidizing the other two to ensure the education of 2,500 students annually.

The foundation also ran the Murugappa Chettiar Research Centre for Rural Development, the goal of which was to provide sustainable livelihood for the poor and marginalized through the use of innovative technology. Edible mushroom cultivation from organic waste was one achievement for the center since it opened its doors in 1977, as well as biomass tech for energy production, and creating safer fishing boats from high-density PE pipes.

"The guiding principle of the Murugappa family is to be firmly committed to what we can do to help the community, and to do so quietly and without publicity," wrote M.V. Subbiah, managing trustee of the A.M.M. Foundation. "Sharing with the community and serving its needs are natural things for us to do—and we just do them."[131]

Then there's the Gordon family of South Africa, members of the Global Philanthropists Circle who are heavily invested in addressing many of the critical challenges that currently face South African society.

---

130 M.V. Subbiah, "A Tradition of Family Giving" *UBS.com*, www.ubs.com/content/dam/ubs/global/ wealth_management/philanthropy_valuesbased_investments/indian-philanthrophy.pdf

131 Ibid.

Donald Gordon, founder of Liberty Group in South Africa and Liberty International in the UK, began the Donald Gordon Foundation in 1971—a charitable trust that is now considered to be "South Africa's largest private foundation and one of the oldest."[132]

South Africa faces many challenges when it comes to charitable giving, not least of which is the stigma that charities in the country are often seen as patronizing. Other issues include the fact that there are no tax incentives in South Africa to encourage the creation of endowments or private foundations, and that the diverse nature of the culture discourages broad-based giving.

The balance, the foundation learned, was in finding ways to financially support true development in the country. Early on, the foundation kept a low profile, working with the disabled and providing welfare for South Africa's Jewish community. Later it launched a Business Science Institute and a Medical Centre, both of which provided modern facilities that train South Africans as potential business and medical leaders.

Although it was not Donald Gordon's first choice to tie his name publicly to so many endeavors, preferring to do his charitable work without recognition, his trustees felt that this practice set an example of family philanthropy and encouraged others to do the same.

"Associating a name with good works has particular meaning in South Africa," stated Hylton Appelbaum, executive trustee of the Donald Gordon Foundation. "And highlighting personal philanthropy in an environment where capitalists are seen as exploiters also signals our commitment."[133]

Charitable contributions, creating trusts, and setting up foundations are IEs that have long traditions in family businesses around

---

132 www.synergos.org/globalgivingmatters/features/0210safamilies.htm

133 www.synergos.org/globalgivingmatters/features/0210safamilies.htm

the world, not only because this is the family's way of giving back to the community that helped it grow, but also because it creates a legacy. By funding charitable efforts that tie closely to family values and by engaging the next generation in the importance of continued contributions to society and the local community, not only is the family strengthened as a unit, but the family legacy is also ensured for generations to come.

I have a reservation when it comes to the idea of legacy, but I find it is the best description in this particular section, in which I chose to focus on family businesses other than our own as there are so many out there, making a difference every day.

Just as valuable as funding the spirit through charitable contributions, however, is funding the mind, and in our family as in many others, education in all its many forms cannot be stressed enough.

CHAPTER 6

Strength in Continuous Education

"Kids can ruin a business."
—ABDUL HAMID BAASSIRI

When I first heard these words uttered by my father upon joining the family business, I was devastated. His statement seemed to come out of left field, and it bothered me so much that I spoke to my relatives about it repeatedly over the next few years.

"You'll understand the meaning of it later," was all they would say.

It was years before I understood what he meant: that experience is invaluable and that no one is entitled to anything … we each need to earn our place in this world. At the same time, I understood that the next generation in family businesses are often given a bigger role to play than they initially earn. To that end, my father decided to set a clear framework from day one, pushing his children to learn and analyze from the collective experience around us and to earn every inch of our place in the family business. It turned out to be one of the best thing he ever did for us.

That education—of learning from experience (including soft tools and reciprocating mentorship) and earning your position—is just as important in our family as formal education, though of the two, formal education used to be less accessible to the masses.

In the late-nineteenth and early-twentieth centuries education—particularly higher education—was an IE in that it was not as available to the general public as it is today. (There is much to be said about today's education and whether or not we should move away from generalized education to more specific skill training. But for now, I'll refrain and speak of the past.) Despite the interruption, my great-grandfather placed an incredibly high value on the pursuit of knowledge, from formal education to life lessons and practical, hands-on experiences earned with your own blood, sweat, and tears. This was the basis for my father's comment about kids ruining business—he saw education as an opportunity to increase wealth and status, and he embraced formal and experience-based education as tools required to succeed in life.

Because of this, A. H. made sure that his only son and all five of his daughters were well educated. It was a unique quality of our family in Lebanon at that time, to have educated daughters, and it has certainly given the following generations a cutting edge, with each generation passing on the value of, and desire for, higher learning.

When it came time for me to find a career path, like most kids my age I wasn't really sure what I wanted. I thought that maybe I would follow in my father's and my maternal uncle's (my father's business partner) footsteps and become an engineer, but my father reminded me that I shouldn't just choose to do something because it aligned with what our family business was currently engaging in. "Do what you love," he said.

I was drawn to becoming a lawyer or a designer, but I chose not to listen to my father's advice and instead chose what I thought of as "middle ground": I shelved my desires and decided to major in business.

It was the new craze in the 1980s. Everyone wanted to be involved in economics/finance, so that's what I did, even though it wasn't what I "loved." It felt a bit generic, but it formed my basic understanding of business, and I expanded on this knowledge by working directly in the business. That time taught me that education doesn't always have to be formal. In fact, no education is entirely formal—you have to learn by doing. Learning in a classroom is only half of the experience, if that.

In fact, "knowledge" as most of us think of it is only a small part of our overall intelligence. There is our intellect, of course, which is our ability to think abstractly and the speed at which we can grasp the essentials and adjust to new situations. But there's also our emotional intelligence and our adversity intelligence.[134] Emotional intelligence is our empathy and compassion, our ability to understand our own emotional state and that of others and respond appropriately. Adversity intelligence, on the other hand, is how well you respond to, withstand, and rise above adversity. Together, these factors are known as Multiple Intelligence Theory[135] and are often abbreviated as someone's IQ (intelligence quotient), EQ (emotional quotient), and AQ (adversity quotient), and to be well-rounded in all three of these should be qualities that any Human Resources department should pursue with a passion. I know that ours does today.

---

134 www.mindecodetd.com/iq/
135 Ibid.

When I started my higher education, however, I wasn't really thinking about developing my EQ, AQ, or even IQ. I was young—at an age when you're not really thinking about anything more than the adventure ahead of you. I completed graduate school before taking a job for a few years outside. Then I decided to come back home and join the family business.

Learning (and Advancing) by Doing

When I came back and chose the family business, I wasn't given a position of authority. I had to earn it, just like everyone else, and that learning started from the ground up.

But that wasn't what I was thinking about when I arrived for my first day of work. I was dressed for the executive suite, with a nice suit on, silk tie, handkerchief, cufflinks … the whole nine yards. I walked up to my father's desk, sat down, and said, "Okay, what's my job description, and where's my desk?"

He looked at me for a second and then said, "You haven't earned a desk, Mr. GQ. You have to learn about the business first."

I was a little surprised, but said, "Okay, so where is HR going to direct me?"

My father's direction was one instruction: to walk around the office and choose which department I wanted to start in. Everyone in our organization had the same instructions—to teach me the basics of their particular branch of the business, what they did and how they did it from A to Z, as far as the general concept.

"At some point, I will decide when you've earned a desk," he said, and with that, our conversation was over.

I went from being Mr. GQ to literally being dressed in overalls. In fact, I still remember one company where I worked in the maintenance department for weeks, wearing red overalls for general work, and blue overalls when I knew I might get grease, oil, and grime all over me.

It was a far cry from the high-status job title with the sophisticated office that I had imagined, but I was learning. Then one fine day, about nine months later, Dad walked over to me, pointed across the room, and said, "That cubicle is yours."

In that first year, I not only learned about our companies from the ground up, but I also learned not to place so much value in status symbols, like desks. It was a concept my father understood more than a quarter of a century before businesses such as Google embraced the idea of "forward-thinking" office spaces based on open floor plans, no desks, and flexible workspaces. Today I don't care about a chair or table or room. I don't care about titles or tables. What's important is what *you* bring *to* the table—what you bring to the processes that can make them better.

During my time in the company trenches, I learned an incredible amount from people who may have been less formally educated than me, but who had far more real-world experience and wisdom. I was able to see the business from the inside out, rather than from a lofty little spot in the sky, and I was able to gain the friendship and respect of the people I would be working with—my team members, our most irreplaceable assets.

This experience was not unique to me alone. Countless other family businesses have seen the value of allowing the next generation to choose their own path and, if they show interest in the family business, teaching them about it from the ground up.

Take the Procacci family in Philadelphia, in the United States. For three generations, the family has run a successful produce business, but becoming a part of the family business isn't a given.

Joseph Procacci III began working on the family farm at age seventeen during the summer, sweeping floors, grading tomatoes, and stacking boxes in the company's tomato-packing house. It wasn't until he really learned about the quality and standards of the company, and watched his father and grandfather oversee the operation, that he decided to become a part of the family business.

Like his father and grandfather before him, however, he earned his role in the company every step of the way. When he wasn't attending Northeastern University for a degree in economics, he was working seventy-five hours a week at the family farm.

"I know I have a lot to learn, and I need to soak up all the knowledge I can from the experienced people inside our company and our industry as a whole," he said in an interview with an industry publication. "I hope I'm fortunate enough to ultimately develop talent and a team to make this company last well beyond my lifetime."[136]

Implicit and Explicit Education

What I appreciated about my early years was that my parents never pushed me to study to fit in at our family business or pressured me to work with our company. My mind-set at the time was that the freedom of choice given to me was an olive branch of trust between my parents and me as I moved from a child to an adult. They considered me to be capable and trustworthy, despite my youth. I had gone to schools and summer camps, traveled on my own already—all as part of a proactive plan by my parents to get me ready for going out on my own—and I'd shown them that I could be dependable and reliable and that I would do well.

---

136 Christina DiMartino, "Next Generation Procacci Learning the Business from the Ground Up," *The Product News*, May 16, 2016. www.theproducenews.com/more-people-articles/people/18766-next-generation-procacci-learning-the-business-from-the-ground-up

But because of this, and other factors, I didn't spend afternoons after school working for any of the businesses our family was involved in. It also meant that I didn't have the opportunity to work anywhere else, either, and learn to appreciate the discipline that such an experience would have offered. Ultimately, my parents wanted me to choose my own path, and my path led me to come back to the business by my own volition.

This was my implicit education. By allowing me to have this sense of independence and giving me permission to seek out what I wanted to do and to discover what I loved, my dad allowed me to experience family first, and I chose the family business instead of feeling stuck with it. He unchained me from that by not chaining me, and I tangled myself in them because I wanted to.

Implicit education—learning by doing—has proven to be a valuable form of learning to many successful entrepreneurs who, for one reason or another, did not receive a complete formal education … a factor that obviously didn't hold them back.

Take Folorunsho Alakija, the second wealthiest woman in Africa as of 2016. The owner of family business Famfa Oil, which discovered one of the largest deep-water oil wells in Nigerian history, she also experienced the IE of never receiving a formal education.

As Alakija told students at the University of Lagos during a 2014 motivational talk, "I never went to a university, and I am proud to say so, because I don't think I have done too badly … You do not have to have a university education to be able to make it, so count yourselves privileged to have that education as part of the feather in your cap."[137]

---

137   Mfonobong Nsehe, "Nigeria's Richest Woman Folorunsho Alakija Reveals She Did Not Go
       To University," *Forbes*, Sept 1, 2014, www.forbes.com/sites/mfonobongnsehe/2014/09/01/
       nigerias-richest-woman-folorunsho-alakija-reveals-she-did-not-go-to-university/#3b0e0fdf10f5

Growing up in her father's store, she learned about textiles and merchandising early on—skills that she later applied to launching a high-end fashion company called Supreme Stitches.[138] From there, it was a matter of keeping her ears open and pursuing opportunities as they arose. From later launching a mass-production t-shirt company to the long struggle to purchase an oil block off the Nigerian coast, Alakija never gave up—not even when the Nigerian government attempted to grab 50 percent of her 60 percent stake in an oil well when she hit that deepwater pocket. It took long twelve years of court battles, but her full 60 percent stake in the company (the other 40 percent belonging to Chevron Oil) was returned to her family.

"Alakija has run a very successful business in Famfa Oil," said Dolapo Oni, Ecobank's Head of Energy Research. "She was one of the first women in the oil business, and her battle with the federal government shows a great deal of tenacity."

Then there's Carl H. Lindner Jr., founder of family business American Financial Group, who dropped out of school at age fifteen to work a milk delivery route during the height of the American Depression, taking high school classes at night.[139] Five years later, he'd opened an ice cream shop with his family and began the process of turning the milk delivery company into what's known today as United Dairy Farmers, a chain of more than two hundred stores selling dairy products and ice cream in the state of Ohio. In 1959, he founded American Financial Corporation (later renamed American Financial Group) and began building a hearty portfolio of controlling interests in groups such as Chiquita, Hanna-Barbera, the Cincinnati Reds, and the former Taft Broadcasting Company.

---

138 Peace Hyde, "How Africa's Second Richest Woman Gained Her Fortune," *Forbes Africa*, Oct 2016, www.cnbcafrica.com/news/western-africa/2016/09/17/africas-second-richest-woman/

139 "Carl H. Lindner Jr. – Cincinnati Business Titan Passes Away at Age 92," *American Financial Group*, Oct 18, 2011, www.afginc.com/phoenix. zhtml?c=89330&p=irol-newsArticle&ID=1618430&highlight=

Because he never finished high school, Lindner was a strong supporter of educational organizations, such as the College of Business Administration at his local University of Cincinnati. According to the obituary released by his company on his passing in 2011, "He liked to joke that his business success was due to the straight-As he earned in his evening high school courses; he found great satisfaction in giving others the educational opportunities he had missed."[140]

As valuable as implicit education can be, however, explicit education can be just as valuable and important to pursue. For my part, explicit education not only involved the career path that I chose but where I ended up following it. My father had gone to school in the West, and I wanted to do the same thing. The actual higher education was only part of it—I also had a strong desire to expand my knowledge of the world and become a "global citizen." What my parents afforded my siblings and I through opportunities to travel and visit new cities and cultures was an educational enrichment made possible by seeing the world from a more global point of view at a young age. I aim to continue doing that with and for my children.

Becoming a Global Citizen

I could have gone to a number of colleges in my neighborhood, but going abroad to seek education meant engaging with other societies, and I aimed to soak in every experience I could, as I did in my travels as a kid with my family, not knowing the impact it would have on my development into a global citizen. I needed to learn as much as I could if later it showed me how to tap into this open approach of continuing to grow our business (be it geographical or otherwise).

---

140   Ibid.

According to *The Economic Times*, "Family businesses, which were once run mostly on practice wisdom and solely by family members, have transformed to more professionally run organizations, and a multicultural exposure appears to be invaluable in being the genesis for reorientation in existing businesses."[141]

Rahul Mirchandani of the family business Aries Agro in Andheri, Mumbai, India, praised his education in Canberra, Australia, where he received his PhD. "India gives you fabulous education, but the life skills that global exposure teaches you are more than education. Global institutes also sharpen your research skills," said Mirchandani.[142]

Since being appointed executive director of his family business in 1994, Mirchandani has been recognized as one of the world's foremost achievers in his field and continues to travel around the world, supporting young entrepreneurs and international relations.[143]

Sue Chen, CEO of NOVA Medical Products, also extolled the value of her education abroad. Born in Taiwan, Chen moved to the United States at the age of four and constantly found herself trying to fit in.

"It wasn't that I didn't fit in anywhere, it was that I didn't know myself," Chen explained in an interview with IES Abroad. "I chose [to study abroad in] Singapore because ... I wanted to speak Mandarin, and I could do that there."[144]

The experience of studying abroad, she added, is something everyone should have. It forces you to become an adult, to get to

---

141 ET Bureau, "Family-Run Businesses Send Heirs for Foreign Education to Sharpen Skills, Lead Workforce," *The Economic Times*, Sept 28, 2012, http://articles. economictimes.indiatimes.com/2012-09-28/news/34148363_1_life-skills-foreign-education-global-exposure

142 Ibid.

143 Aries Agro, "About Us" page, www.ariesagro.com/BoardofDirector.html last accessed Oct 4, 2016.

144 "Sue Chen, CEO, NOVA Medical Products, Singapore, Fall 1990," *IES Abroad*, Fall 1990, www. iesabroad.org/study-abroad/alumni/profiles/sue-chen#sthash.xN2vUH6m.Dryec0Cj.dpbs

know yourself and learn how to be flexible and adapt to new situations. It also taught her the valuable lesson of seeing the world from more than one cultural standpoint.

"Going to a country that is very different and has very different rules, it makes you think about things in a different way. Whether right or wrong, the world has different perspectives," she said.[145]

Together, her experiences taught her how to form connections with all kinds of people, learning from them and establishing relationships that have benefited the growth of her family's business.

"There is a skill set you develop when you are abroad ... a confidence and a courage and a fearlessness that starts becoming part of your wiring when you're in a new place and begin experiencing new adventures. Today, as a business leader who wants to make change, it requires this fearlessness and courage. I absolutely attribute those experiences in Singapore to learning all those things you need today to run a company, or to be successful, in whatever way you define it," said Chen.[146]

I am certain that both Mirchandani and Chen's experiences, and mine, are but an indicator of the numerous benefits earned by travel-abroad education. What lies ahead for the next generation is endless opportunity not only around the world but also beyond, as travel evolves from terrestrial to interstellar.

Education Never Stops

Regardless of whether you were formally educated or learned from the ground up, whether you work for a company, joined the family business, or started your own, to be successful you need to seek knowledge and to educate yourself. It could be as simple as taking

---

145   Ibid.

146   Ibid.

the time to read an article, a book, or even watch a documentary. You need to aim to learn something new everyday. And if you are lucky enough, you get to learn from those who came before you, just as my father taught me about the life lessons he'd learned over the years we worked together, and as I learned from a collaboration of great minds in Palo Alto about our potential for the future. (For more on Forward Thinking, see Chapter 8.)

I believe the best life lessons I was taught came from working with my father rather than just visiting him or hearing stories from him in a casual context. I discovered how he dealt with our business in the past because he went through the same things I was going through and set a high standard for me to follow in the process.

He didn't talk about past glories or spilled milk. The past was just that—the past—in his eyes. Instead, he talked about the lessons to be learned, such as forgiveness and giving and the continuity of self-improvement.

In family business, a big part of your education is in how to work well together as a family, which is an exponential lesson you will never stop perfecting. To be a husband and wife is hard work; to have children and raise them is hard work; to actually continue that relationship and closeness is hard work, and to do that across different branches of the family through multiple generations is hard work—and that's not even factoring in the family business on top of all that!

But one thing I've come to understand, which is reinforced almost every day, is the value of sticking with your family no matter what. You can't just let them go. You can't "plug in" and "plug out" of your family, only seeing them during the holidays and not calling or visiting the rest of the year, and still expect the same degree of mutual understanding that only comes from a strong relationship.

That's a value that is dying in so many ways across the world, but it is one of the keys that allows family businesses—and families—to survive.

That isn't to say that we should allow ourselves to become insular. As much as families can grow together and become a place of comfort and tradition, as I alluded to earlier, you must also allow yourself to be open to other cultures, other traditions, and new diversity. By not bringing in new blood, new challenges, and younger team members with different core values and principles, you become stagnant. Invigorate your business—update yourself by infusing new and bright ideas into your processes. The learning curve dies after a certain cycle unless you invest in education and diversification. No one has all the answers, but you can see through many more eyes by consistently bringing in fresh perspectives.

Allow the known as well as life disruptions. Diversify as you would in business and that mentality will serve you well in both your family company and your family itself. All the education in the world isn't worth much if you can't relate and grow and learn outside of your own comfort zone.

In the end, if you've worked to cultivate your relationships, if you've been open to learning from new and differing points of view and educating yourself on how to balance work and home, if you've worked toward diversifying your world perspective, then you'll find that your education has paid off. This collective will be there for you, and together you'll make it through the best and worst of times.

Education and Equal Pay

One can't discuss education, however, without mentioning the female journey. Regardless of whether their studies are conducted at home or in foreign countries, the number of women partaking of higher education is increasing rapidly worldwide. Since the 1970s, average global university enrollment for women has increased from a ratio of 62.5 percent women per men to 107.5 percent women per men as of 2014.[147]

In fact, according to a Yale report, the number of women enrolled in higher education exceeds that of men in two out of every three countries.[148] And women are outnumbering men in graduation rates worldwide, with women making up the majority of university graduates in countries such as Argentina, Nigeria, and Iran, and are coming close to equal in graduation rates in the world's largest two populations, China and India, at 48 and 42 percent, respectively.

Even so, the developing world still faces its fair share of struggles in reaching gender parity in education. In sub-Saharan Africa, and south and west Asia, for instance, roughly one-third of the female population's education is interrupted by child marriage (marriage before the age of eighteen). However, UNICEF states that "if all girls had secondary education in sub-Saharan Africa and south and west Asia, child marriage would fall by 64 percent, from almost 2.9 million to just over 1 million."[149]

In the GCC, women are rapidly closing the gap both in education and in positions of power in family businesses. In fact, a 2015 study stated that "family businesses in the GCC will have more women on their boards over the next five to ten years as they transition to the third generation of control."[150]

---

147   Joseph Chamie, "Women More Educated Than Men But Still Paid Less," *YaleGlobal*, March 6, 2014, http://yaleglobal.yale.edu/content/women-more-educated-men-still-paid-less-men

148   Ibid.

149   "Girls' Education and Gender Equality," *UNICEF*, www.unicef.org/education/bege_70640.html, last accessed Nov 7, 2016

150   Andrew Scott, "Women Are the Next Family Business Leaders in the GCC," *The National*, Jan 21, 2015, www.thenational.ae/business/economy/women-are-the-next-family-business-leaders-in-gcc

The study went on to state that women are now outnumbering the number of men graduating from higher education in the GCC, and an increasing number of women are pursuing degrees in law, engineering, business, and the sciences.

Looking back over the past forty, fifty, even one hundred years, women's progress in education has certainly come a long way, but, sadly, the idea of equal pay has not. Even after all this time, the annual pay for women worldwide is still far behind that of men, with women on average earning the same annual salary that men earned ten years ago[151]—a gap that isn't expected to reach economic parity for another 170 years as of 2016.[152]

Fortunately, however, more family businesses are supporting equal pay, including Gap Inc., a family-owned company since 1969, which recently signed the United States White House's 2016 Equal Pay Pledge. In its pledge, Gap Inc. stated, "In 2014, Gap Inc. became the first Fortune 500 Company to announce that we pay female and male employees equally for equal work on average across our global organization. This is an important step globally, as well as in the U.S., where a woman earns on average 79 cents for every dollar a man earns. When we pay our employees fairly and treat them with dignity and respect, they are inspired to be their best, which in turn helps us deliver better products and experiences to our customers. And when our business succeeds and grows, we can become a stronger voice for equality and inclusion around the world."[153]

Our company supports equal pay for men and women, and we encourage all businesses, family or otherwise, to do the same.

---

151 *World Economic Forum Global Gender Gap Report 2015,* http://reports.weforum.org/global-gender-gap-report-2015/

152 Al Jazeera report, "WEF: Gender Wage Gap Will Not Close for 170 Years" *Al Jazeeera,* Oct 26, 2016, www.aljazeera.com/news/2016/10/index-gender-wage-gap-close-170-years-161026071909666.html

153 "These Businesses Are Taking the Equal Pay Pledge," *White House.gov,* www.whitehouse.gov/blog/2016/06/14/businesses-taking-equal-pay-pledge

Our next chapter looks at gender empowerment in family-owned businesses.

CHAPTER 7

Gender Empowerment

"A man who treats a woman like a princess, must have been raised by a queen."
—ATTRIBUTED TO THE *MANUSMRITI*

When my daughters were five, seven, and nine years old, they said something to me that at once opened my eyes and filled me with shame. As worldly and open minded as I thought I had been until that day, in one sentence they showed me how I had unknowingly been wearing spectacles of prejudice for decades.

One of my passions is collecting historical documents, and I'd just added a new piece to my collection when the girls came into my office. I was so excited to show them everything hanging on my walls.

"Look at these," I said. "These are historical documents that tell you about change." And I pointed out the letter from Mahatma Gandhi, and the one from Martin Luther King Jr., another one from Albert Einstein, and one from Thomas Edison. I showed them a document from Abraham Lincoln, and even a letter that former President Jimmy Carter wrote to me.

"See," I said to them, pointing to Gandhi, Einstein, and Martin Luther King, Jr., "here's a Hindu, a Jew, and a Christian, and all of them were working for peace."

I started to explain Einstein's regret over his contributions to the atomic bomb, and Gandhi's peaceful resistance, babbling on and on in my excitement over sharing the collection and my collected knowledge.

Meanwhile, the girls were just looking up at the wall curiously. When I finished, they simply looked at me and said, "Are only men famous in history?"

I was stunned. This whole time, the fact that my treasured documents were only from men never even occurred to me, even though I had a very strong role model in my mother and grandmother. I had been completely blind to the fact that I was living in a male-focused bubble, but with one question, my daughters completely altered the way I saw the world. It was as if I had never been able to see the color blue until that day.

Soon after that, I embarked on looking for documents from famous women to add to my collection. Today, I have a document from Marie Curie, who pioneered research into radioactivity, and another one from Rosa Parks, the famous civil rights activist. I even have a signed picture from Valentina Tereshkova, the first woman to fly in space, and the search goes on to seek Saint Theresa and others.

It's a start, but it took the untainted eyes of my young daughters to make me realize how easily I brushed over the accomplishments of historically famous women in favor of men. But that insight made me dig inside myself to realize the incredible value of every woman in my life, from my late grandmother to my mother, my sisters, my wife, my daughters, my female colleagues, and so many others.

Even as the world has progressed in terms of equality, to this day both on the broader social scale as well as in business, women continue to struggle with the IE of gaining leadership roles in business. However, family businesses seem to be doing a better job than most of supporting female executives (just look at 1,300-year-old family business Hoshi Ryokan welcoming its first female owner), with a 2014 survey of family businesses worldwide finding that 70 percent are considering a woman for their next CEO.[154]

The reasons for this trend, according to the report, is due to a number of factors, including an increased interest by women in joining the family business, as well as the direct benefit of the tendency for companies "with the greatest number of women in the c-suite outperform[ing] on return on equity and other financial performance metrics."[155]

Julie Smolyansky, for instance, didn't exactly have shareholders' complete confidence when she took over the family's kefir business, Lifeway, following the IE of her father's sudden death. At twenty-seven years old, she remembered her father's best friend telling other shareholders to sell their stock because "there's no way this girl can run a company." Some left, but those who stuck with her and the company were rewarded. In 2013, under Smolyansky's leadership, the company topped $98 million in sales, and the company's stock is up 785 percent since she took over.[156]

---

154 "Staying Power."

155 Ibid.

156 Karsten Strauss, "Women, Leadership, Matt Lauer, and Taking Over a Family Business: Julie Smolyansky Sounds Off," *Forbes*, June 29, 2014, www.forbes.com/sites/karsten-strauss/2014/06/29/women-leadership-matt-lauer-and-taking-over-a-family-business-julie-smolyansky-sounds-off/#29422021764c

"There's a lot of sexism that exists all across the board," said Smolyansky. "I think that diversity is magical, and that's where the strongest teams happen."[157]

In Latin America, Carmen Ferrao is the CEO of marketing and sales for her family's company Lojas Pompeia,[158] a chain of more than seventy family fashion shops in southern Brazil.[159]

A graduate in social communication, management, and retail, Ferrao was asked by her father to help create a new marketing plan for the company soon after she graduated at the age of twenty-six.

"The main barriers to women in business are the ones they erect themselves," said Farrao. "I had to understand that I was capable and that I had my own way of working, and from that perspective, it was easier to deal with any prejudices I encountered."[160]

As the first female CEO of her company, Farrao has become a role model not only for women in her industry but also for women throughout Brazil.

In the GCC, obstacles to women in the workforce have historically included a patriarchal society and lack of education, according to a 2015 study,[161] but growing trends toward more educated females in the workforce and social acceptance of women in senior roles has helped to boost the number of women in positions of power.

Take Muna AbuSulayman, Saudi Arabia's Goodwill Ambassador and cohost of the Middle East Broadcasting Center's popular social program, *Kalam Nawaem* (*Speech of the Soft*). She is considered a

---

157 Ibid.

158 www.lojaspompeia.com/institucional#historia

159 Jane Simms, "Latin America: 'Si Senora' Ladies Take the Family Business Lead," *Campden FB*, Nov 1, 2007, www.campdenfb.com/article/latin-america-%E2%80%9Csi-se%C3%B1ora%E2%80%9D-ladies-take-family-business-lead

160 Ibid.

161 Scott, "Women Are the Next Family Business Leaders in the GCC."

strong supporter of women's empowerment around the world as well as in Saudi Arabia, a place at the cusp of change.[162]

In an interview with *Arabian Business* in 2010, AbuSulayman stated, "When you change women's conditions and empower them, you change the whole family."[163]

HE Ohood Al Roumi is also breaking new ground as the first Minister of State for Happiness for the United Arab Emirate. Appointed in February 2016, she continues to hold her office as director general of the Prime Minister's Office of the UAE, as well as serve as the vice chairman of the World Government Summit Organization.[164,165] In fact, at the time of her appointment, she became one of five women to be appointed to the UAE cabinet by UAE Prime Minister HH Sheikh Mohammed Bin Rashid Al Maktoum.

Ellen Johnson Sirleaf, too, made her mark in Liberia in 2006 when she became the first female head of state in modern African history.[166] Winning the vote against soccer icon George Weah, Sirleaf was supported in force by women voters, paving the way for future female African presidents, including Catherine Samba-Panza, interim president of the Central African Republic in 2014; Joyce Hilda Banda, president of Malawi from 2012–2014; and Ohsan Bellepeau, acting president of Mauritius in 2012 and 2015.[167]

---

162 https://en.wikipedia.org/wiki/Muna_AbuSulayman

163 Anil Bhoyrul, "Foundation for Change," *Arabian Business*, Nov 1, 2010, www.arabianbusiness. com/foundation-for-change-358822.html?page=2

164 www.happy.ae/en

165 Alexandria Gouveia, "Minister of Happiness Has Been Revealed...And It's a Woman," *Emirates Woman,* Feb 10, 2016, http://emirateswoman.com/minister-happiness-revealed-ohood-al-roumi/

166 Lydia Polgreen, "In First for Africa, Woman Wins Election as President of Liberia," *New York Times,* Nov 12, 2006, www.nytimes.com/2005/11/12/world/africa/in-first-for-africa-woman-wins-election-as-president-of.html

167 Ricky Riley, "7 Female African Presidents You May Not Know," *Atlanta Black Star,* Sept 22, 2105, http://atlantablackstar. com/2015/09/22/7-female-african-presidents-people-may-not-know/2/

And then there's Peng Lei (also known as Lucy Peng), one of *Forbes's* 2016 most powerful women in the world. Cofounder of online marketplace Alibaba and founder of Alibaba offshoot, Ant Financial Services, a company that specifically serves small business, Peng led her company during the largest privately held fundraising drive for an internet company in 2016, raising $4.5 billion and bringing the company's value up to $60 billion.[168] As of 2015, Ant had more than 450 million active users and had extended more than 20 million small- and micro-loans to both entrepreneurs and small businesses.

Throughout the world, women are moving into positions of power, from Michelle Bachelet, the first female president of Chile in 2006; to Jóhanna Sigurðardóttir, the first female prime minster of Iceland appointed in 2009;[169] Umu Hawa Tejan-Jalloh as Sierra Leone's first female Chief Justice in 2008; and Pratibha Devisingh Patil, the twelfth president of India, from 2007 to 2012.[170] Even in 1921, women were being recognized in leadership positions, with Khertek Anchimaa-Toka serving as the Head of State of Tannu Tuva, now the Tyva Republic in southern Siberia.[171]

The issue of gender parity has even become one of the leading topics in the business world, with the 2016 World Economic Forum addressing the issue as one of its top discussion points, along with climate change and refugees.[172]

---

168 Kane Wu, "Alibaba Affiliate Ant Financial Raises $4.5 Billion in Largest Private Tech Funding Round," *Wall Street Journal*, April 25, 2016, www.wsj.com/articles/alibaba-affiliate-ant-financial-raises-4-5-billion-in-largest-private-tech-funding-round-globally-1461642246

169 Michael Ray, "Johanna Sigurdardottir," *Encyclopaedia Britannica*, Nov 23, 2015, www.britannica.com/biography/Johanna-Sigurdardottir

170 https://en.wikipedia.org/wiki/Pratibha_Patil

171 http://www.guide2womenleaders.com/Presidents.htm

172 Jennifer Openshaw, "Lack of Women Still a Hot Topic at Davos," *CNBC*, Jan 25, 2106, www.cnbc.com/2016/01/25/lack-of-women-still-a-hot-topic-at-davos.html

"Men have a unique opportunity in this, as we still make up 80 percent of the executive ranks and even more than that at the CEO level," said Mercer CEO Julio A. Portalatin during the forum. "We have a unique obligation to be out in front on growing women in the workforce. It's not a women's issue: this is a workforce issue."[173]

And as Coca-Cola CEO Muhtar Kent pointed out during the same forum, "We need the three Ws: women, water, and well-being."

"It's hard to ignore the mounting evidence that more gender-balanced leadership teams correlate with better business performance," said Kate Barton, vice chair of Tax Services for EY Americas. "There are fascinating studies of the different ways in which women and men assess risk and make decisions that reinforce the conclusion that promoting gender equality is just smart business. I'm not suggesting that one is right and one is wrong, but diversity leads to balance, and balance—particularly when considering risk—is healthy business."[174]

It is the same thing my late father said for so many years: "Hold things in the middle."

In fact, that same survey found that "companies with the greatest number of women in the c-suite outperform on return on equity and other financial performance metrics," noting that women on company boards tend to focus more on issues of risk reduction and governance—both of which underpin superior financial results.

And yet, women in powerful leadership roles continue to deal with the challenges of being a woman in business. Advancement is consistently difficult, regardless of whether you are in business or a family business.

According to a 2016 report by the American Association of University Women (AAUW), "Women are much less likely than men

---

173   Ibid.

174   "Staying Power."

to be in leadership positions," despite the fact that they "earn the majority of university degrees at every level except for professional degrees." The report goes on to point out the gender disparity in leadership positions, from the US Congress (81 percent male, 19 percent women) to executive roles in the United States, with white men currently holding 63 percent of the executive seats.[175]

And then there is the finding that, as of 2015, there are more S&P 1500 firms run by men named John then there are female CEOs—a sad indicator that women are still struggling to attain leadership roles in the corporate world.[176] As much as we like to think that gender bias is a fading issue for our enlightened generation, these numbers—and the real struggles they reflect—tell a different story.

Take, for example, A.B.,[177] who develops platforms for her family business and assists shareholders in the decision-making process, as well as directs the structure of another company's governance holdings and handles the consolidation of its financial information, business strategy, and its development for next generations.

"It was not easy to get here," A.B. said. "It was a challenge to earn my position because of my gender. In my role at a different company earlier in my career, I had to fight to earn the professional respect of an executive who worked with me, a sexist man who thought that women should stay at home and take care of the house and children. That's how many family businesses operated for generations, but we also know how much businesses change over generations.

"As a female in the business world, you have to be super competent, resilient, and a warrior, because things will be much

---

175 AAUW, "Barriers and Bias: The Status of Women in Leadership," *AAUW.org*, March 2017, www.aauw.org/files/2017/03/barriersbias-one-pager-nsa.pdf

176 Justin Wolfers, "Fewer Women Run Big Companies Than Men Named John," *New York Times*, March 5, 2015, www.nytimes.com/2015/03/03/upshot/fewer-women-run-big-companies-than-men-named-john.html

177 Due to the potentially controversial nature of their statements, A.B., R.T., and S.K. have asked to be identified by their initials only in this book.

harder for you than it will be for a man. You need to learn how to deal with people and try to find a well-balanced lifestyle."

A.B. faces the IE of gender inequality every day, and as much as I work to empower the women around me, both in my own family and the women in my company, the difficulties inherent to the gender gap continue today to rear their ugly heads. "Some men don't like women as their boss, but when we're able to reach a point of understanding and cooperation, it can be a good team," stated T.P., a female forum member of mine who plays an integral role in her family business. "Women should do what they love, first. They should be able to purse their dreams freely." As for our own female family firm members, I would say their contribution is to be noted, as I am lucky to be surrounded by their strength and intellect.

According to my sister, a board member in our family business, "As much as we like to think that gender inequality is a thing of the past, that we're an enlightened generation that treats each other fairly, for females the fact is that fairness in gender equality is still yet to be achieved. I experienced it earlier while working in continental Europe, and I still experience it today in my day-to-day interactions. Women are not given the same opportunities, are still paid less,[178] and are still subjected to the same outdated stereotypes, such as our ability to balance both work and personal life.[179] The result is that women still have a much steeper hill to climb if they're hoping to one day hold an executive or c-suite position. Change will not come easy, it will require a well balanced reboot but it will come."

"There have been strides and achievement for women in the Gulf, this I cannot deny," said R. T., CEO of a large firm in the UAE.

---

178 "Pay Equity & Discrimination" Institute for Women's Policy Research, 2017, https://iwpr.org/issue/employment-education-economic-change/pay-equity-discrimination/

179 Fishel, Allegra, "Gender Discrimination in the Workplace" New York Times, August 15, 2010, https://mobile.nytimes.com/2010/08/16/opinion/lweb16mothers.html

"We have women as ministers, and women have a large percentage of representation in the public sector. We have women accepted in the family business. However, in family business, the common practice and thought is that even if the woman is the eldest sibling, it is the brother that will be groomed to lead."

"Being a woman CEO has challenges, and the social challenges are quite bothersome," R. T. added. "There haven't been many I've seen that have been able to break the chain of predetermined destiny, of tribally bestowed positions, and an almost nonexistent concept of merit, so the chain tightens until we bleed. Some grow nasty and bitter, and some just give and conform."

There are questions that arise again and again, said R. T., such as whether or not we are happy, or satisfied, or whether we really know what it is that makes us happy. The questions don't apply just to women, either, but to both genders.

"Even though the society we are discussing is patriarchal, we do fall into the trap of assuming that women can actually ask these questions," said R.T. "Society has dictated what happiness should be for my gender. If we choose to pursue another path of realization, the pioneers would be chastised and their children will feel the wrath. Until we become a society that truly respects every individual thought and ambition regardless of gender, we will still have gaps in the mountain we will be climbing."

In an interview with *The Atlantic*, Farida Jalalzai, author of *Shattered, Cracked, and Firmly Intact: Women and the Executive Glass Celling Worldwide*, said, "We have to acknowledge that men are not faced with the same suspicion that they can't be good leaders simply because they're men. Tomorrow someone might say that President Barack Obama was a complete failure, but no one is going to conclude that all men are bad leaders. So, there's a certain type of privilege that your success or failure is not going to reflect on your entire sex."[180]

Another successful entrepreneur and friend, S. K., shared her thoughts with me on the challenges of climbing the ranks in business.

S. K., who is the director of marketing, communication, and purchasing at her family's company, found that one of her greatest difficulties was in overcoming the emotion of being the daughter of the boss and a colleague of the men on staff.

"Learning how to communicate effectively with them, particularly with the older generation, seems to be a magnificent challenge due to gender, and gaining their trust in order to earn a promotion was harder still," said S. K. "Society has a different expectation for women in business. If I were to give advice to any woman looking to take on a powerful role at a company, regardless of whether it's their family's or a business in general, I would tell them to do what they love, first. Everything should come from doing what you want to do, not what other people want you to do."

"Pursue your dream freely," is something that I tell my daughters as often as I can—that, and how I promise to be there for them through all of their highs and lows in life.

In spite of the multitude of challenges that women have faced and continue to face in business, such as in the example of the above where the challenge did not deter them, they are successes in their own field. Women have historically held significant roles in family businesses, in some cases even saving the business from complete collapse, though they rarely received the recognition they deserved.

Take Elizabeth Durtnell of the construction firm R. Durtnell & Sons. This family business is now in its thirteenth generation, but it

---

180   Sharamilla Ganesan, "What Do Women Leaders Have in Common?" *The Atlantic*, Aug 17, 2015, www.theatlantic.com/business/archive/2016/08/what-do-women-leaders-have-in-common/492656/

very likely wouldn't have made it this long if it hadn't been for Anne Durtnell, nee Langridge, a woman that the family commonly refers to as "The Iron Woman."[181]

Following the untimely death of her husband and family business leader Richard Durtnell in 1856, Anne took over running the company with an iron fist, in some cases "visiting Durtnell building sites on horseback, haranguing foremen for wasting time and materials, and ordering workmen to pick up dropped nails," according to the Durtnell's Family Tree. She wasted nothing, accounted for everything, and when she died in 1892, she was buried in an iron casket.

Because of Anne, the family business survived through generation eight and is considered as sturdy and well-built as the first home the Durtnell family built in the 1590s: Poundsbridge Manor, which still stands today in Penshurst, Kent, England.[182]

Another family business that owes its survival to female family members is Pizzini Wines of Australia.

When first-generation Roberto Pizzini arrived in Australia in 1955, it was with the goal of building a better life for himself and his growing family. On reaching northeast Victoria, Roberto, his wife, and their three children dug potatoes for a living until they'd saved enough to start growing tobacco on a farm shared between Roberto and his two brothers.

Eventually, the tobacco farm was split between the three brothers, and Roberto's son, Alfredo, began planting grapes. Today, the Pizzini vineyard is 170 acres of grape production consisting of seventeen different varietals, and the quality of their wine has played a signifi-

---

181 R. Durtnell & Sons Limited Building Contractors, "The Family Tree," http://durtnell.co.uk/index.php/history/family-tree

182 R. Durtnell & Sons Limited Building Contractors, "Durtnell's 1st Building," http://durtnell.co.uk/index.php/history/durtnells-1st-building

cant role in seeing the King Valley of Australia become a recognized and respected wine-growing region.

Through it all, Alfredo credits the influence and management skills of both his wife, Katrina, and mother, Rosa.

"Originally, Dad did everything, basically," said Alfredo in an interview with family business researcher Laura Hougaz.[183] "Katrina was busy raising the family. But you can't achieve these results on your own, that's impossible. ... Once the kids grew up, Katrina herself started taking over the administration, which then meant that I'd spend more time outside, growing the business. ... They [his wife Katrina and mother Rosa] are strong women, they are strong and they are correct, and they are accurate in what they choose to do and how they perform in whatever they are doing. In terms of the business itself, they have a huge, huge strength. They are part of the business."

Whether through blood or marriage, females continue to fight for influential positions in family businesses.

Caroline Lubbers, for instance, developed her skills outside of the family company before joining the fold and making her mark. Lubbers, the daughter of two people involved in family businesses, followed her own path by working for Hilton in Italy before returning to her mother's family business: Hotel Theatre Figi in Zeist, Netherlands.

On joining the family firm, Lubbers took up the role of marketing manager and eventually earned her way onto the family board.

"Female leadership is different than male leadership," said Lubbers.[184] "My mother used to tell me about when she started out in business and how she was the only woman among many men.

---

183 Hougaz, *Entrepreneurs.*

184 *Great Expectations.*

Things have changed since then, but I think women still need to find their own leadership style and have the confidence to follow that through."

Lubbers faces several challenges in her position, not least the challenge of marketing in a digital age, but feels that her family firm should focus on the long-term profitability while allowing itself to be reinvented with each new generation, adapting products and services to what the market demands. As long as the company's core values are followed, the family firm can benefit from this fresh approach.

Along with her work with the family's business, Lubbers also runs a social enterprise business focusing on cocoa and chocolate that relies on an international network of women for its success. "Because empowering women is, and always has been, the best way to achieve real, positive change."[185]

The Gender Balance

"We do not only empower women, but we empower the whole community through women."
—PRIME MINISTER OF THE UAE,
H.H. SHEIKH MOHAMMED BIN RASHID AL MAKTOUM[186]

There have been many, many reasons for the lack of women in family business leadership roles, not the least of which has been the lack of confidence on the part of the men in the family and their unwillingness to pass over the reins to what they may wrongly consider the "weaker sex." At the same time, however, research has shown

---

185 Ibid.

186 "We're Proud of Emirati Women: Leaders," UAECABINET.ae, https://uaecabinet.ae/en/details/news/were-proud-of-emirati-women-leaders. Last accessed July 11, 2017

that some women still sadly grow up with a lack of confidence in themselves.

According to a PWC survey[187] on the next generation in family business, females are more likely to believe that the males of their generation are expected to take over the business, with 44 percent saying that they hope to manage the family business compared to 67 percent of men. At the same time, only 77 percent of women believe that their family has confidence in their ability to lead the company. Compare that to the belief that 93 percent of men have their family's confidence regarding their leadership ability, and you have a significant gap in confidence levels.

And yet, women appear to be more welcome in leadership roles in family business than they are in the corporate environment at large, according to a joint survey conducted by EY and Kennesaw State University's Coles College of Business in 2015.[188]

"The increased interest implies that inclusive leadership and the concern for others and their opinions displayed by the gender balance of these businesses tend to create a sense of belonging that, in turn, builds trust and engagement," the report states.

Marilyn Carlson Nelson, co-CEO of Carlson Holdings and former CEO of worldwide travel and hospitality company Carlson, is an excellent example of women taking powerful roles in family business. According to Nelson, her father, Curtis L. Carlson, "was absolutely crushed" to only have two daughters and no male heirs. But he still taught her about leadership, including the valuable lesson, "If you don't like it, fix it." [189, 190]

187 *Great Expectations.*

188 "Staying Power."

189 Marilyn Carlson Nelson bio, *Carlson.com*. www.carlson.com/cdc-cms/pdf/Bios/Marilyn percent-20Carlson percent20Nelson percent20Bio.pdf

190 Keren Blankfeld, "Women on Boards of Family Businesses," *Forbes*, May 11, 2015, www.forbes.com/sites/kerenblankfeld/2015/05/11/women-on-boards-of-family-business/#7f0097d73130

Not one year before her father passed away in 1999, Nelson took over as CEO of Carlson—a $35 billion business consisting of more than 550 Radisson hotels, 600 TGI Fridays, 470 Country Inns & Suites, and numerous ventures, including real estate and travel.[191]

At the helm of Carlson, Nelson not only drove the company's continuing growth but also its humanitarian efforts, cofounding the World Childhood Foundation with the Queen of Sweden to protect homeless children across the globe, and taking a stand against human trafficking and child sexual exploitation in the travel industry.[192] She has been named by *U.S. News and World Report* as one of "America's Best Leaders" and by *Forbes* magazine as one of "The World's 100 Most Powerful Women."

And then there's Indra K. Nooyi, CEO of Pepsi-Co and number 14 on Forbes's "The World's 100 Most Powerful Women" for 2016.[193] The mother of two, Nooyi joined Pepsi-Co in 1994 and became president and CFO in 2001. In 2006, she became Pepsi-Co's fifth CEO and has steadily increased the company's annual net profit from $2.7 billion to $6.5 billion since 2001. But she's also a mother, and balancing that life has been a challenge for her, just as it is for all working women. In an interview with Atlantic Media owner David G. Bradley, Nooyi frankly pointed out that, "I don't think women can have it all. We pretend we can have it all. Every day you have to make a decision whether you're going to be a wife or a mother. In fact, many times during the day you have to make those decisions."[194]

---

191 Carlson Holdings History, www.carlson.com/our-company/history.do

192 Marilyn Carlson Nelson bio, Carlson.com. https://www.carlson.com/cdc-cms/pdf/Bios/Marilyn%20Carlson%20Nelson%20Bio.pdf

193 "Indra Nooyi, 'The World's Most Powerful Women 2016,' *Forbes*, www.forbes.com/profile/indra-nooyi/

194 Conor Friedersdorf, "Why PepsiCo CEO Indra K. Nooyi Can't Have it All," *The Atlantic*, July 1, 2014, www.theatlantic.com/business/archive/2014/07/why-pepsico-ceo-indra-k-nooyi-cant-have-it-all/373750/

She added, "Being a stay-at-home mother was a full-time job. Being a CEO for a company is three full time jobs rolled into one. How can you do justice to it all? And the person who hurts the most through all of it is the spouse. My husband, Raj, always says, 'You know what, your list is always Pepsi-Co, Pepsi-Co, Pepsi-Co, our two daughters, your mom, and then at the bottom of the list is me.' And I always tell him there are two ways you can look at it: you can see yourself at the bottom of the list, or you can be happy you're on the list."[195]

Women in family business not only face all of the challenges that males face, but they are also under the additional scrutiny that unfairly falls on them due to their sex. In our family business, we strive to walk the talk. Women hold several of our top leadership roles, be it family members or team members, and we are adamant about equal treatment. But, as we have found, this is not the case for many businesses. Fighting against such an imbalanced system is a difficult task to undertake, and it is one in which education plays a key role (see more about this in Chapter 6), but those women who do take it on gain a powerful asset that will serve them well as they successfully guide their family business toward the future.

---

195 Ibid.

CHAPTER 8

Forward Thinking

"If you always do what you always did, you will always get what you always got."
—ALBERT EINSTEIN

At the end of a long talk with my father about the importance of raising responsible kids, I remember sharing with him how I recollect from an early age how I embraced the importance of planning and reevaluating plans early on, creating my first five-year plan at the age of nine (don't judge!).

"My mind is full of plans as far as the eye can see," I told him proudly. And I would continue on with those plans until I reached the age of seventy, at which point I would sit back and take it all in and enjoy life.

I told him that story with such optimism, but as I finished, my father wasn't smiling. Instead, he looked very thoughtful. After a moment, he said, "I am sixty-six years old. So according to your plan, I can't sit back and enjoy everything I've done with my life for another four years?" he chuckled.

The way he put that jolted me. I realized that I had been so focused on the next thing that I was missing the moment. I was doing too much forward thinking and too little living in the moment. I needed a different plan going forward. It was a turning point for me, another abrupt interruption reminding me to stop and take in the small moments. Like in some of my other non-work endeavors, including hobbies, I seemed to be at a loss on how to "play hard." It comes down to just enjoying my time, from walks on the beach to group adventures. Although I missed being part of it, I admired my T2T gang for the trip they took during the summer of 2017, bicycling from the Eiffel Tower to the leaning tower of Pisa. I can't help but mention how inspired I was by everyone on that trip, including my dear friend Abdul Rahman Al shathry AAA); they just lived in the moment. As the saying goes, "Healthy mind, healthy heart." Working out was that starting point, something I always enjoyed; running, swimming…even more so with my trainer and friend Craig Dunham (a Rolf method practitioner[196, 197]) who shared with me the "Rolf Method" process, from which I learned how to ground myself in the here and now, to stand upright with grace and ease, and allow the earth to give me support. As I said, it is a starting point.

The importance of this was made even clearer to me when I shared the idea of this book with Bassam Soueidan, a dear friend of mine. He liked the idea of "forward thinking" but pointed out that the book was missing a part about living in the moment. He reminded me that today is not something we can get back, that we

---

196 www.craigdunham.com

197 www.rolfguild.org

need to enjoy the time we have, and we need to teach our children to do the same. He has since passed away in June 2017, and ever since we spoke, I've been reminding myself to try and live each day in the present, be grateful, and seek balance of mind, body, and soul. Like most of us, I still yo-yo in and out of this profound gift of advice that he shared.

Appreciating the Present, Planning for the Future

Looking at our present-day family business, I can't say what the future will look like, but I do know our business is likely to change … and that is because it has done so in the past. Over the past one hundred-plus years of our family business history, the longest business cycle activity has been this one, which has lasted a little more than forty years.

This is true for any long-running business. Business cycles change. Just look at the number of iconic brands that shone so brightly in the past and then faded, even though the company that made them is still going strong. Volkswagen's Beetle, for instance, was an icon of the 1960s that fell out of popularity until most sales stopped in 1979.[198] After a nearly twenty-year hiatus, the model returned with a major redesign and survived until 2011, when an even newer New Beetle, the A5, was released. With each cycle, VW proactively rode the rise and fall, focusing on the present while preparing for the future, a future where the current auto industry is gearing toward another IE—a technological one unlike anything we have seen before.

Instead of bracing for, and reacting to, change, we should accept it as inevitable and approach it proactively. In our family business,

---

198 Alexander Stoklosa, "The Bug's Life: A History of the Volkswagen Beetle," *Car and Driver*, www. caranddriver.com/flipbook/the-bugs-life-a-history-of-the-volkswagen-beetle

we expect our business cycles to end eventually, which is why we created an investment fund (as I mentioned in an earlier chapter) that encourages the generation of new ideas and promotes better communication. The fund is one of the strongest tools we have to counter the concern over what the future might hold and when that next business cycle may begin.

In embracing the flexibility, entrepreneurial nature, and global citizenship of our past, we have been able to move from one place to another, from one business to another, conducting our present business as we also plan for the future—a new kind of future that we may have yet to envision.

Forward Thinking in Palo Alto

Seeking some insight on the possibilities of the near future for *all* types of businesses, not just family, and recognizing that the technological revolution is in full swing (and has been for over half a century), I attended a Singularity University conference in Palo Alto, California, organized with the help of my buddy Devon Capur, in October 2016 on the subject of artificial intelligence, or AI, among many intriguing and interesting topics about exponential growth and change.

What the conference reconfirmed was that, yes, you can do anything you put your mind to, as there is a place and time for everything (as my mom instilled in us). What, really, do you want to put your mind to? What possibilities can you imagine? What IEs are out there that we have yet to face? This isn't about reinventing the wheel; it is about tossing the wheel out altogether and looking at what the word "to move" means in the first place. Forget vulcanizing rubber to produce superior rubber tires—why not transport organic matter as quickly and easily as you make a phone call? Why not turn the phrase "Beam me up, Scotty" into reality?

To move forward, I found, means to look beyond convention and simply assess the raw materials, the raw question that you need to answer.

Take the words, "Take me to the moon."

What seemed impossible fifty years ago? To today's disruptive technology, where the question is, "How do I get there?" The answer is closer than ever. You could soon purchase passage on a space shuttle to the moon, or you could take Elon Musk's approach and build your own spaceship. Or you could do what my brother did—sign up to go on Richard Branson's Virgin Galactic, where you'll get a closer look at the moon and spectacular view of earth from sub-orbit.

Talk about a one hundred thousand foot view, where space and time are infinitely connected and where true imagination has no limits. To move forward on any question requiring innovation, we need to tap into that imagination, look at the situation's most basic elements, and consider the solution simply from that perspective and what really is possible. Do we need bulky spaceships, or do other possibilities exist?

The concept of first principles, though it applies so well to the rapid advancement of technology, has been around since the time of Aristotle. They're the basic assumptions, the self-evident propositions that cannot be derived from anything else.

"We need energy," for instance, or "I think, therefore I am." Once we understand the basic elements we're working with, we can look at it from another angle: same materials, new path. Why make a better wheel when you can abolish the wheel altogether?

Take the traditional medical doctor, for example. In the old days, the doctor used to come to your house and see how you were, give you a shot or prescribe you medicine, and would come back and check on you in a few days later to see how you were doing. As transportation became faster and more readily available, however, and as cities became more centralized, that tradition disappeared. People drove to the doctor and waited their turn.

But now that's changing once again. What's old is new again as doctors "come to your home" via your computer or mobile device. They can offer diagnoses, prescribe medication, and even perform surgery remotely, making the expertise of highly specialized surgeons available globally.

Same elements, new path; and the possibilities are growing exponentially.

First Principles and Changing the Way You Do Business

In the 1990s, a young Iranian emigrant named Sahar Hashemi was lamenting to her brother about the lack of low-fat options in the cafes around her home in London.[199] Sahar, a lawyer, and her brother Bobby, an investment banker, had recently lost their father and were both questioning their chosen career paths. But as Sahar spoke, both realized that she'd voiced a desire in their community that was likely shared by thousands.

The coffee chain craze hadn't gained much of a foothold in the UK when Sahar and Bobby launched the Coffee Republic chain in London, which quickly grew to more than one hundred outlets across the UK.

It was an incredible success, but as the chain grew, the Hashemis became disenchanted with the concept and eventually sold it in 2001. But the original elements that sparked that first entrepreneurial con-

---

199 "The Bred Entrepreneur," *Global Citizen*, May 23, 2016, http://global-citizen.com/the-bred-entrepreneur/

versation still hadn't faded from Sahar's memory. Instead of walking down the same path and launching another chain, Sahar turned the interruption to her advantage and began a low-fat candy-making company called Skinny Candy in 2005. In the meantime, Bobby went another direction, taking the elements of the chain concept and applying them toward opening a pizza chain called Pizza Union.

Both businesses have been successful, with Sahar selling Skinny Candy two years after launching it and focusing instead on a career as an author and speaker, intent on letting people know that becoming a successful entrepreneur is something anyone can do.

"Legend and conventional wisdom have made us believe that unless you are a swashbuckling extrovert who has loved business since kindergarten (preferably making your first million selling sweets in the playground) and are somehow blessed with otherworldly skills, then starting up on your own is not an option. ... Rubbish. All sorts of people start businesses and all sorts of people thrive after doing so," writes Hashemi in her inaugural book, *Anyone Can Do It.*

One of the most important things to remember, she adds, is that you should never become so set in your ways that you miss new opportunities.

Just as digital entrepreneurs such as Google and Netflix have shown us in recent years, and established companies such as Berkshire Hathaway have proven by evolving from a textile industry in the 1950s to global investments, *there are no limits to reinventing yourself.*

Take Wipro Technologies, an IT services company based out of Bangalore, India, that turns over billions of dollars in revenue every year, earning it the nickname "IBM of India."[200] But as its name suggests, Wipro was not always in the IT industry.

---

200   Dave Roos, "10 Companies That Completely Reinvented Themselves,"*money.howstuffworks.com,* 10 January 2014, http://money.howstuffworks.com/10-companies-reinvented-themselves.htm

Founded in 1945, Wipro started out by selling vegetable oil, hence its name: Western India Vegetable Products. Over time, the company took on selling other household products, such as detergents, soaps, and talcum powder, but in 1966, when Azim Premji took over the business from his father, he caused an IE for the company when he took a whole new direction by opening up an IT division. As of 2014, Wipro commanded $6.9 billion in revenue, with more than half of that coming from the United States for R&D and IT consulting—and they still sell household products, too, just under the name Wipro Enterprises Limited, a story I can relate to.

Our company has evolved a lot over the years, and each new venture adds more depth, character, and diversity to it.

I spoke earlier in the chapter on funding about struggling to start my own independent company and how fortunate I was to be embraced as part of the family business. It so happened that about six years after we launched, the company was given the opportunity to execute a project that was challenging but didn't feel like the most challenging project we'd ever done. When we finished it, however, we were surprised to receive an award for executing the single largest order of this product in the world: a 4,000-unit single order delivered at one time and through multiple contractors.

It was an honor but also a great tribute to the way in which our entire company had evolved. That individual ventures can conduct their work on world-changing scales speaks not only to our ability to change how we do business but to be able to take things down to their elements and look at how tasks that might seem complicated in their present state may be done differently and better from a new angle and by taking a new path.

Complacency Is Death

"All the companies I've worked for have this deep problem of devolving to something like the hunting and gathering cultures of 100,000 years ago. If businesses could find a way to invent 'agriculture,' we could put the world back together and all would prosper."

—ALAN KAY

According to Wayne Rivers, cofounder and president of the Family Business Institute, "The seeds of a successful family-owned business's destruction are sown in good times." He later adds that, "Complacency is a death sentence for a family business."[201]

Both true, and both true not only for family business but for business in general. There is a multitude of examples to pick from: companies that were once household names that have since become little more than ghosts, such as Circuit City, Kodak, and Nokia.

Nokia, for instance, has sadly become well known for its CEO's last words when he announced the company's purchase by Microsoft: "We didn't do anything wrong, but somehow we lost."[202] Even though the mobile phone company was the first to introduce smartphones in 1996, they failed to see the value of software over hardware and relied on their name power to carry them, while companies such as Apple and Android began to dominate the field.[203] In the end, they weren't able to keep up with the pace of innovation, and the result was the end of a brand that once held claim to being one of the most valuable brands in the world.

---

201 Wayne Rivers, "When Does a Family Business Begin to Fail?" *Family Business Institute*, www.familybusinessinstitute.com/when-does-a-family-business-begin-to-fail/

202 Rahul Gupta, "Nokia CEO Ended His Speech Saying This: 'We Didn't Do Anything Wrong, but Somehow, We Lost,'" *LinkedIn*, May 9, 2016 www.linkedin.com/pulse/nokia-ceo-ended-his-speech-saying-we-didnt-do-anything-rahul-gupta

203 James Surowiecki, "Where Nokia Went Wrong," *The New Yorker*, Sept 3, 2013, www.newyorker.com/business/currency/where-nokia-went-wrong

Missed opportunities and failures to turn interruptions in entrepreneurship toward positive change abound in the business world, with examples such as Blockbuster famously turning down the purchase of Netflix in 2000 for $50 million—a company that was valued at more than $32 billion only fifteen years later[204]—or Verizon turning down a chance to carry the first Apple iPhone, allowing Apple to join forces with Cingular.[205] I wonder what we will say about Apple in five years' time!

Kodak, too, had its chance at continued success and yet turned it down out of nearsighted fear.[206] Despite inventing the first digital camera in 1975, the company failed to market it because of the potential negative impact on its film industry (no pun intended). In thinking it could protect its profits by stifling technology, Kodak instead left the door open for others to take over the burgeoning digital film industry. The seeds of its demise were sown at a time of great success.

"Immensely successful companies can become myopic and product-oriented instead of focusing on consumers' needs," wrote marketing strategist Avi Dan in a 2012 *Forbes* article.[207] "Companies have to adapt to the requirements of the market, even if that means competing with themselves. Technology has the potential to be disruptive of markets and companies at the same time that it is benefiting consumers. … In this environment, marketers should strive for entrepreneurial greatness and innovation, not to just determine preference among existing options."

---

204 Celena Chong, "Blockbuster's CEO Once Passed Up a Chance to Buy Netflix for Only $50 Million," *Business Insider*, July 17, 2015

205 Rob Beschizza, "Verizon Turned Apple iPhone Down," *Wired*, Jan 29, 2007, www.wired. com/2007/01/verizon_turned_/

206 Avi Dan, "Kodak Failed By Asking the Wrong Marketing Question," *Forbes*, Jan 23, 2012, www.forbes.com/sites/avidan/2012/01/23/ kodak-failed-by-asking-the-wrong-marketing-question/#1dd490777dd7

207 Ibid.

Value Creation and Destruction

"If at first the idea is not absurd, then there will be no hope for it."
—ALBERT EINSTEIN

As family business owners and members of family businesses, we need to think beyond the box we have put ourselves in or actually inherited—the preconceptions that have crusted around us as we've grown older—and break it all down. We need to break outside of the mental prison that we're in and constantly be thinking about "what's next," no matter how successful we may be at any one time.

In the 1920s, the average lifespan of a company listed in the S&P 500 was sixty-seven years.[208] By 2012, that average lifespan had dropped to a mere fifteen years. Global markets are one hundred to one thousand times larger than they were in 2000, due to increased global reach, and both the cost and time it takes to develop new technology has dropped dramatically.

The rate of change in business is growing exponentially, and technology is one of its strongest drivers.

Just look at Moore's Law, for instance, which states that the number of transistors that can fit on a square inch of integrated circuits doubles every two years. At some point, due to heat emanating from the transistors, technology would reach its limit. However, even though that statement has held true since Intel cofounder Gordon Moore first said it in 1965, it is now being challenged as the tech industry looks beyond transistors toward even more advanced means

---

208   Kim Gittleson, "Can a Company Live Forever?" *BBC*, Jan 19, 2012, www.bbc.com/news/business-16611040

of electronic thought, from the Deep Learning chip[209] to reconfigurable chips known as FPGAs.[210]

As quickly as new tech rises, it is outpaced by even newer tech—and the time frame between one innovation hitting the market and its better replacement is getting shorter and shorter. Value is being destroyed almost as quickly as it is being created, which can be good for a business that's staying on its toes and constantly looking ahead for "what's beyond what's next," but it is the death of any business not willing to look beyond its present success.

It is hard to look beyond the known. As much as we may tell ourselves that we need to think beyond how well our company is doing today and plan for future opportunities, it's much easier to stick with the path that we're familiar with. Disruption is uncomfortable, but it's necessary if we're going to evolve.

This mind-set is one of the many reasons I appreciate our diverse team. One can get stuck in their comfort zone because they see the same things every day and revolve in the same circles. Therefore, one needs an extra set of eyes looking at the company from other angles and letting you know where your weak links are and where you can grow. Of course you won't always agree, but that's healthy; it means you're being challenged. This is important in order to refrain from remaining stagnant and ultimately leading to your own demise. As Mahatma Gandhi said, "Honest disagreement is often a good sign of progress."

Controversial thoughts are where innovation thrives. They were the origin of the telephone and the car, the airplane, and spaceships. By asking questions, by thinking beyond the given and looking at

209 Nicole Hemsoth, "Deep Learning Chip Upstart Takes GPUs to Task," *The Next Platform*, Aug 8, 2006, www.nextplatform.com/2016/08/08/deep-learning-chip-upstart-set-take-gpus-task/

210 Margaret Rouse, "Field-Programmable Gate Array (FPGA)," *WhatIs.techtarget.com*, Sept 2005, http://whatis.techtarget.com/definition/field-programmable-gate-array-FPGA

the possible (or even the impossible, because who's to say what's impossible today won't become possible tomorrow?), we grow, and in growing, we thrive—from a horse carriage, to a car, to hyperloop, to even being beamed up. Every business, in essence, is a dream focused on the wish for success and recognition. Innovation often comes from the desire to love what we do—and in creating that passion, we create something new.

There are times when the nature of interruptions is such that there is no need to reinvent the wheel, just find new uses for it. But with today's ever-evolving technology and fast innovation, the need to think outside of the box, to break out of your own mental prison, is becoming more important than ever as a means to deal with disruptive interruptions. We should be going past the idea of the wheel itself and asking if there's even a use for the wheel anymore. Is there a better solution?

POSITIVE THINKING

While on its surface this book is about family business, its deeper meaning is about goals, about change, and about not waiting for other people to push you to move forward. I shared this advice with my three daughters in a poetic form (more an "attempt for poetic form ") some years ago, and—in the spirit of the book to share lessons while trying them in a new form—I am putting myself out there and showing a side of me that most people don't get to see:

Life is like a river
It runs fast and slow
Wide and narrow ...

Meander down the river with your goals
Remember ... Goals will evolve, they are just part of the whole ...
Be flexible while you stand tall
Be willing to duck to weather the storm

Sometimes the wind doesn't even blow ...
You must get up and push forth
To see what the future holds

Armor yourself when you open your arms
To moments of happiness and others of grief
cushion life's tidal waves
By Wearing your heart, sometimes, within your sleeves

Aim to improve, Think Big, and Get in the drivers seat.

To my daughters, Faye, Talia, and Lana
— Raméz A. Baassiri, your loving dad

I am grateful for all that I have seen:

My father, soaring up in Heaven,
Looking down to earth on my mother, who is a beacon of giving;
My Siblings, who have my back twenty-four seven;
My loving wife, who is positively driven;
My three wonderful children;
I count my blessings and what I have been given,
A slice of Heaven.
— Raméz A. Baassiri, observer

In this book, I allude to cultivation, land, and planting. Each of us is given a plot of land—life—to garden, grow on, and cultivate as we will. We may leave it dry or overwater it, but we ought to plant multiple seeds that we wish to grow in it, and work to care for those seedlings so that they can mature into productive plants. Trees and vegetation, like goals, grow in different environments and at different paces. Ideally, we give each what it needs.

I look at my plot of land as a starting point that could be made into anything. I learn as I go, and as I plant more seeds, I may find that I'm better at growing some things than others, that other plants grow better here or there, and in this learning, I evolve and grow, as well. Some areas I'll plant seeds to harvest in the short term; some sections I'll plant seeds that will take years to mature, such as wisdom and patience. And there will be seeds that are more difficult to grow, that I have to learn to cultivate by experience. Each part of the garden needs to be nurtured in different ways, and how I go about that, how I plant and tend and plan out my garden, is what makes me who I am.

We live in a world of more abundance, more choices, so we need to be more focused and decipher what we need or want to get out of life, our plot of land.

How is it that we live in a time of more but have less time to enjoy?

What is important is the knowledge and good values we have and can share. This is what earns one a good reputation.

Plowing through the Plants

I use the garden analogy often in my thoughts and sometimes with my children, too. Whenever I'm learning something new, I just tell them that I'm "plowing through the plants," because in learning, I find that even when old roots might need to be torn out, the soil around it is ready to infuse life in the next planting. No garden is ever going to be perfect. One corner might get a return on investment far faster than another, and another may not return anything at all, but it looks incredible to you.

The lesson of all of it is that no matter what type of garden you grow, no matter what interruptions you confront, you have to put in effort and time. You have to work in the blazing hot sun and the rain, go through the seasons, and learn from each of them, and you will have to understand what each and every one of your plants requires, and keep up with them.

Flowers may bloom for a season and be gone forever, others may last years, but one day they, too, return to the earth, so you must plan for it and plant always. In that sense, you are constantly reinventing and updating yourself. It's an effort, but it teaches us patience and appreciation and to wait for things that need a little more time.

You don't get a twenty-foot-tall tree in a day, but if you're willing to put the work in and get started today, you'll be that much closer to having one down the road—if not for you, then for the next person down the line.

Hard Work, Strong Bonds

To be together as a family, both immediate and extended, is hard work. And to actually continue those relationships and that closeness is even harder work. To do that across different branches of the family in multiple generations is even more hard work, but at the core of it, your success is in your strong bonds. Invest your time and effort in them and I am certain it will be time well spent. There are times when it's not all that rosy, when things start to go pear-shaped, that is when your investment will reap you unimaginable support through the worst life can throw at you, because you took the time to be there for them. But I know to some this may not be true as connections with others may be hard to attain. The key message is: have someone to love, and who loves you.

This kind of thinking—of keeping up with bonds and communicating not only because you need something from them, working on those bonds that are withering away—is so important to cultivate. You must be able to forgive the person in front of you, you must try to be there for them when they need you, and hopefully that drives them to want and do the same … be the first to genuinely offer an olive branch. It is worth the effort.

This is why you still have such strong families in places like Germantown and Chinatown in melting-pot countries such as the United States. Places where whole families have immigrated, often only a few family members at a time until everyone—aunts, uncles, cousins, nieces, nephews, and great-everythings—are together and sharing their culture, their food, and their religion with other families from the same areas, often with others whose family branches intertwined with theirs at some point in the past several hundred years. That is not to say that an even stronger tie can be the blending of different ties.

As these threads weave together, becoming stronger here and branching out there, creating this amazing tapestry of family and work and life, we all find ourselves in our unique moment in time, looking forward. Several generations ago, our forefathers saw the rise of industry and embraced that interruption as a change that could catapult their families forward into the bright new future - and we continue to do the same today. We stand in our moment and celebrate the incredible interruptions and opportunities that technology and artificial intelligence will bring us. We embrace the future as we do family - with open and welcoming arms, happy for the present and looking forward to all the things we will achieve going forward.

Look beyond the Familiar

That's not to say, however, that we should limit our worldview to just our family and the environment we are raised in. There is great value in knowing your neighbor, but there is even greater value in knowing all of your neighbors. And not just knowing them in a superficial way but in a way that you find comfort in being around them, even when they don't act like you or talk like you. To know your neighbors, as diverse and as many as possible, is to add value and depth and texture to your own garden.

Keep your family close but always look at the present and toward the future with an eye focused beyond the familiar. Have a plan for your garden, plant and tend as you will, and know now that probably 70 percent of what you plant won't actually come to fruition as you thought it would—and that's okay. By planning and working with the whole world in mind instead of just a small slice of it, you avoid the potholes and detours of going down the wrong roads. Allow for new things, new experiences. The world will reward you, and your garden will flourish.

Thank You

I would not be able to conclude this book without thanking my mother and letting her know that my courage to write this book stems from what I learned from her experience in writing her own literary works, including poetry.

And to my father, I can only hope that he knows not only how much I learned from him, but how I continue to learn from him today. Thanks to the wisdom and the farsighted vision that he shared throughout his life, I approach every day thankful for what it brings and for what the future holds.

Finally, thank you to the team that helped me bring this book to life, including Kristin Hackler, George Stevens, Eland Mann, Adam Vlach, Megan Elger, Keith Kopcsak, Kirby Andersen, Katherine Beck, and the rest of the team at Advantage.